READER IN A STRANGE LAND

Reader in a Strange Land
The Activity of Reading Literary Utopias

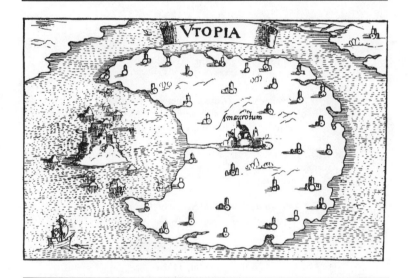

PETER RUPPERT

The University of Georgia Press: Athens and London

The paper in this book meets the guidelines for permanence and
durability of the Committee on Production Guidelines for Book
Longevity of the Council on Library Resources.

The illustration on the title page is from the 1612
German edition of Sir Thomas More's *Utopia.* Courtesy
of Historical Pictures Service, Chicago.

Printed in the United States of America
90 89 88 87 86   5 4 3 2 1

Library of Congress Cataloging in Publication Data

Ruppert, Peter, 1941–
Reader in a strange land.

Bibliography: p.
Includes index.
1. Utopias in literature.   I. Title.
PN56.U8R86   1986   809'.93372   85-16512
ISBN 0-8203-0821-8 (alk. paper)

for Jeanne

Contents

Preface

Utopias," writes Michel Foucault, "afford consolation: although they have no real locality there is nevertheless a fantastic, untroubled region in which they are able to unfold; they open up cities with vast avenues, superbly planted gardens, countries where life is easy, even though the road to them is chimerical."[1] Foucault's description effectively sums up what must be considered the dominant perception of utopias and indicates at the same time why they are so often dismissed. Conceived of as one-dimensional dreamworlds, utopias delineate unearthly visions of peace and perfect harmony, homogeneous regions of order and precision and happiness, that seem to provide us with comforting reassurance. In the process, they appear to ignore difference, to reduce multiplicity and diversity, and to exclude choice, conflict, complexity, history. So, as Foucault suggests, the consolations they bear are in fact illusory, the easy solutions they offer are false, and the assurances they provide are no assurances at all, only escapist dreams that oversimplify the way things really are.

And yet, in spite of their apparent reductiveness and their devotion to unity and order, utopias leave us with a productive sense of uneasiness and ambivalence. To begin with, the very sites that utopias construct so meticulously to sustain their visions of order—the blessed isle or happy future—are by definition unreal and unreachable: they are "no-places" in space and time and there are no actual roads that we can travel to get there—only "chimerical" ones. But these "chimerical" roads are constructed from the discarded bricks of our own failed social institutions and real social misery. Utopias may exist nowhere, but their critical value can be seen to exist in their capacity to defamiliarize and draw attention to real social problems. Where they may fail to convince us of the sufficiency or the finality of their sanguine solutions, they also fail to dissuade us from the need to search for social alternatives. Where they demonstrate their own inevitable flaws, their own blind spots and failures, they inspire us not with derision and a sense of futility but with the desire to envision social and political arrangements that can correct the flaws, illuminate the blind spots. And where they remind us, again and again, of the irreducibility of some social conflicts, the inescapability of certain opposing claims built into the nature of social life, they nevertheless challenge us to examine these opposing claims in the hope of finding a possible solution.

Utopias have these critical effects because the texts in which the "untroubled regions" are delineated are structured on an open-ended dialectic, an ongoing dialogue between voices expressing what is possible and what is necessary in human affairs. Utopian literature, it seems to me, has always proceeded on the basis of this dialectic, but the implications of this dialectic for the reader have not been sufficiently elaborated. Recent reader-oriented literary theory and criticism provides us with an opportunity to investigate the extent to which utopian literature invites the dialectical involvement of its readers, the extent to which it relies, for its full realization, on the responses of readers to the dialectical structures embedded in the texts themselves.

My purpose in this study is not to determine what utopias mean, but to examine how they can mean different things to different readers. Like other literary texts, utopias are structured to produce certain effects in the process of reading them,

to move their readers in certain ways. Structured and organized as dialogues, utopias set out to engage their readers in a
dialogue on social alternatives and social variations. What initiates this dialogue is the experience of noncoincidence between social reality and utopian dream, the incongruence between what is and what might be or ought to be. This
noncoincidence produces thoughts, stimulates desires, makes
us dissatisfied with the way things are. In envisioning these
desires, utopias attempt to produce a disturbing and startling
effect: they invite us to entertain social alternatives, to open
ourselves to other possibilities, to make the process of reading
an occasion for discovery about the social world in which we
live. Seen this way, reading utopias can be an activating experience, an experience that undermines our social beliefs, modi-
fies our social values, changes us. In a genuine dialogue, of
course, both sides can be changed; but even though reading
cannot provide us with this kind of genuine dialogue (since
there is no opportunity for spontaneous interaction), it is nevertheless a twofold act, the product of a dialectical interaction
between reader and text in which one affects the other: the
utopian text directs our thoughts and channels our desires, the
reader performs the text, materializing its intentions and messages; the meaning that emerges from this transaction is the
bridge established between these two sites.

The impetus for this study of literary utopias comes in a
general way from the recent "rediscovery" of the role of the
reader in literary theory and interpretation, but in a more direct way it emerges from the renewed critical interest in utopian literature and utopian discourse evidenced in a number
of important works that have appeared since the 1960s. Together, these developments challenge us to rethink some of
our basic assumptions about utopian literature and to question some of our procedures in its interpretation and evaluation.

The mood that characterizes recent studies of utopian

thought is cautious and restrained, indicating that the utopian fervor of the 1960s and 1970s—the peace movement, the counterculture, the various communal experiments, the popularity of utopian writers like Herbert Marcuse, Paul Goodman, Norman O. Brown, Allen Ginsberg—has given way to a period of calmer reflection and critical inquiry. It may be ironic that this critical interest in utopias comes at a time when utopian enthusiasm and utopian action are generally seen to be in a period of decline; but this may also be an appropriate development in view of the extravagant and exaggerated claims made on behalf of utopias in the past. At any rate it is a sober attitude that informs such recent works as Frank and Fritzie Manuel's historical study *Utopian Thought in the Western World* (1979) and Louis Marin's provocative rereading of More's *Utopia* in "Toward a Semiotic of Utopia" (1978). Where Marin provides us with an exhaustive method of reading utopian narrative, the generic studies of Darko Suvin ("Defining the Literary Genre of Utopia" [1973]) and Gary Saul Morson (*The Boundaries of Genre* [1981]) identify textual structures and narrative strategies that help us to account for the unsettling effects that utopias can produce in readers. Their findings are exemplified and substantiated, as we shall see, in the open-ended utopias of H. G. Wells, Marge Piercy, and Ursula K. Le Guin. In these ambiguous utopias, the imaginary no-place is no longer represented as a homogeneous "untroubled region" of timeless social harmony, but as a region that is itself insufficient, incomplete, and open to change. These "heterotopias," to use Foucault's term, are intentionally inconclusive so as to engage the reader as a more active participant in the ongoing process of producing utopian variations.

A number of these studies suggest that, rather than one-dimensional blueprints for social reform or consoling visions of identity, utopias are better understood as open-ended interrogations of social reality that are themselves contradictory and inconsistent. The basic presupposition of these studies is that utopias should be grasped as works of the imagination, as symbolic constructs, which function not to represent islands of social perfection but to serve as thought-provoking catalysts whose value is in their shock effect on readers. If we approach utopias this way, then they become reader-oriented works that call for an acutely dialectical perception on the part of the reader: rather than uncovering social problems and formulating easy solutions, utopias may now be understood to delineate incompatible images of social life in order to draw attention to the discrepancies among them and to intensify our perception of these differences.

Overall, my barely submerged chief concern in this study is to defend utopian literature and to demonstrate its continuing relevance. No doubt my own priorities, predilections, and biases as a reader are evident enough. The objectivity of this book may be imperiled by the fact that I provide an admittedly incomplete survey of the great variety and diversity of utopian literature and by the tendentious way in which this survey conforms to my own views. I will be more than satisfied, however, if this study causes its readers to reconsider their attitudes toward utopias and to question the assumptions with which they evaluate utopian literature. For it may just be, as Fredric Jameson has suggested, that it is not so much utopian literature that has become "obsolete" today as it is "a certain type of reader, whom we must imagine just as addicted to the bloodless forecasts of a Cabet or a Bellamy, as we ourselves may be to Tolkien, *The Godfather, Ragtime,* or detective stories." Jameson goes on to suggest that our current low regard for utopian literature and our basic distrust of anything "utopian" may be due less to the many limitations and shortcomings of the basic texts of this genre than to the disappearance of this reader, now replaced by a reader of another sort, whose "fantasy tolerance is . . . modified by a change in social relations: so in the windless closure of late capitalism it [has] come to seem increasingly futile and childish for people with a strong and particularly repressive reality-and-performance principle to imagine tinkering with what exists, let alone its thoroughgoing restructuration."[2] Utopias have always implied such a "thoroughgoing restructuration"—and readers who are willing to entertain its possibilities.

My procedure in the chapters that follow is to survey the various readings of utopias on the basis of the literary and ideological assumptions that inform them and to demonstrate the latent possibilities that a dialectical reading of these texts can reveal. I begin in chapter 1 with a description of the contradictions that characterize utopian literature and that account for the different kinds of readings that utopias have received. In chapter 2, I survey these approaches, illustrating how readers with different priorities and different critical procedures have read utopias in different ways. In chapter 3, I propose a way of reading utopias based on their dialectical structures. Chapter 4 examines Louis Marin's exemplary reading of More's *Utopia* and focuses on the contradictions in More's text. In chapter 5, I argue that anti-utopias are not so much efforts to discredit utopian values as they are, in terms of their effects, an extension of the utopian narrative strategy to inspire the reader with concern and unrest. In chapter 6, I show how certain "ambiguous utopias" are intentionally open-ended in order to make the reader an active participant in the ongoing process of restructuring utopian values. Chapter 7 concludes with suggestions for the most appropriate way of deriving the significance of utopian literature. Taken as a whole, these chapters are intended to illustrate the problems and decisions inherent in the activity of reading utopias as well as to provide some answers—answers that are, in the nature of those contradictory utopian solutions themselves, necessarily provisional and inconclusive.

1

Introduction
Readers in Utopia

I understand, said Glaucon: you mean this common-wealth we have been founding in the realm of discourse; for I think it nowhere exists on earth. No, I replied; but perhaps there is a pattern set up in the heavens for one who desires to see it and, seeing it, to found one in himself. But whether it exists anywhere or ever will exist is no matter; for this is the only commonwealth in whose politics he can ever take part.

— *The Republic of Plato,* TRANS. F. M. CORNFORD

The activity of reading literary utopias, as this study is subtitled, might suggest a fairly straightforward and limited process. Utopias are, after all, such simple and direct representations: they employ the conventions of realism in order to map out (usually in vexing detail) ideal and perfect social arrangements to which the reader is asked merely to assent. Their content, moreover, is so reductive and stereotyped that, for many readers, utopias are easily dismissed either as one-dimensional blueprints for socialism or as harmless escapist fantasies. Either way, their critical impact on readers seems minimal. As models of peace and social harmony, they generally fail to inspire readers: few utopian ideals are realizable or even desirable, and no utopian scheme has ever been fully implemented. As fiction or

1

fantasy, the basic texts of the genre are considered dull and constraining: they lack the irony and complexity of the more modern forms of fiction that we have come to valorize. The prevailing view of utopian literature is that it is much too didactic, programmatic, and coercive, and that the only "activity" it allows for the reader is her unquestioning compliance with or conversion to utopian values.

Indeed, from our perspective today, the whole concept of utopia must seem antiquated, inadequate, and hopelessly naive. We feel generally uneasy about utopian claims and assumptions—particularly the claim that socialism or communal ownership of property will eliminate a myriad of social ills—and we question the basic premises upon which utopias are constructed. In reading utopias, we find it difficult to suspend our disbelief, since life within the boundaries of these imaginary communities is presented as disconcertingly serene and uncomplicated: social relations are always harmonious, ethical conflicts are always minimal, everyone we meet, it seems, is always smiling, content, and happy. The basic assumption upon which this perfect happiness is based is that a change in social relations will change human nature itself, a change in political arrangements will produce a different kind of person—one who is kinder, more generous, and more cooperative. On this unconditional premise, utopian writers construct images of order, simplicity, and human fulfillment. Their firm belief is that existing social relations can and ought to be changed; thus, they envision an imaginary time or place in which the desired changes are abruptly "realized," then proceed to construct barriers and boundaries against further changes. For most readers, this procedure raises more questions than it answers: How can human nature be changed so easily? Exactly how are these remarkable changes to be accomplished? Can the conflicts and violence of history be dissolved so easily? If human beings are capable of living together in such harmony and mutual cooperation, how is it that in all recorded history we never find them doing so?

In spite of our severe doubts and misgivings, we are nevertheless drawn to these irrepressible visions of hope and optimism. We are fascinated, first of all, by the variety, diversity, and resilience of the utopian imagination, which has produced such a rich and enduring tradition. Among its diverse products we find maps of ideal cities and elaborate architectural projects; political tracts, treatises, and manifestoes; ideal constitutions and detailed blueprints for educational reform, marriage, and communal life; and novelistic descriptions of fictive communities. We sense a unifying principle behind this great diversity—the recurring human desire for peace, happiness, and community—and we admire the boldness of these visions in opposing existing standards, values, and norms. Taken at their best, these visions dare to entertain alternatives that constitute a significant departure from the status quo, thereby giving indirect expression to our deepest conviction—that we are more than what our historical situation allows us to be, that we have not yet realized our full potential as human beings. By providing us with more rewarding and more fulfilling images of social life—images of human solidarity and more genuine human relationships—utopias hold out the possibility that we are able to go beyond the more familiar experiences of anxiety, fragmentation, and alienation.

At the same time, however, when we consider these cloudless visions more carefully, we find that they also testify to our inability simply to dream our way out of our historical situation. Implicit in all utopian dreams is the urge to escape, the desire to get away from the turmoil of history and the anxiety that comes from an awareness of time and change. Hence, those ever-present boundaries that enclose all utopian landscapes. We can understand the motivation behind this urge for separation and exclusion, but we question the

3

efficacy of this desire, the power to realize the dream it envisions. Indeed, the immense gap that separates dream from reality is perhaps nowhere more evident than in the experience of reading utopian literature. What strikes us again and again in reading utopian works is precisely the incompatibility between utopia and history, a recognition that, in terms of practical results, these visions have been powerless and ineffectual. Looking backward over the centuries of utopian thought and expression, we find that, for the most part, these dreams have lacked any hope for realization and seem destined to remain forever on paper. Even those actual utopian communities that were founded on utopian principles—New Harmony, Amana, Oneida, and so forth—never quite realized the ideals that inspired them and ended, usually, in dismal failure.[1] It seems apparent, then, that the great majority of utopian dreams and visions have been politically and historically ineffective. Utopia remains, by definition and by design, an image of "other" possibilities, a form of social life not as it ever was or ever will be, but only as it might have been or ought to be. In short, utopia—the image of a good society that is "nowhere"—is discontinuous with history; it can exist only in discourse and is realizable "nowhere" except in the imagination.

In view of this fundamental rift between utopian dream and social reality, our ambivalence and doubts about utopian literature seem more than justified. What possible value can these sanguine visions of social perfection still have for us today? What functions, if any, do they perform? Has utopian literature become an obsolete and irrelevant form of social speculation? What is the efficacy of utopian desire if its impact on history is so decisively negligible?

We can attempt to answer these questions by examining the ways in which utopian literature has been read and interpreted, that is, by investigating and assessing how its functions and meanings have been inferred by readers. For

4

the efficacy of utopian literature lies neither in its capacity to inspire actual social reform nor solely in its status as a form of fiction. Instead, the importance of these works lies in their disturbing and unsettling effects on readers, that is, in the very ambivalence and doubt they arouse in us. For in spite of their apparent simplicity, their naive assumptions, and their formulaic solutions, these texts continue to generate diverse and at times contentious responses. No matter what our social attitudes and political convictions are, utopias try to make us aware of countervalues, counterattitudes, counterpositions. Utopias set out to challenge existing social values, to undermine existing norms, to transform existing social beliefs. They engage us in a dialogue between social fact and utopian dream. What initiates this dialogue is the recognition of contradictions and disparities: the noncoincidence between social reality and utopian possibility, the incongruity between "what is" and "what might be" or "what ought to be," the discrepancy between history and utopia. The effectivity of literary utopias, the central experience and most important effect of these texts on readers, is a sharpening of our perception of these contradictions and disparities—confrontations of opposites that seek to ignite a fertile clash in the reader's mind and to arouse his own utopian desires.

My main concern, then, is with the pragmatic or functional aspects of utopian literature: how these works engage us and position us as readers attending to their arguments and messages, how they may activate and liberate us in this process or how they may leave us passive and complacent. In taking up this issue, I will examine the potential effects of literary utopias, both in terms of how these effects have been inferred by various readers and how I think they ought to be inferred. My view, essentially, is that utopias are best understood in the context of a dialectical model of the reader/text relationship—one in which the reader's position is not entirely in the text, nor entirely outside it, but alternates productively between

5

these positions. In such a dialectical approach, reader and text are inextricably bound together: the activity of the reader is elicited by the text, and the text cannot be realized in the absence of the reader's performance. But it is, ultimately, the reader who is the site of productive activity, the point at which meaning is produced, and the reader's participation determines to a large extent the kinds of effects that are realized in the act of reading.

Literary utopias, we will see, emphasize the reader's role as an active producer of meaning: they invite us to enter into a dialogue with the text and to formulate a meaning that may not be explicit in the text, but which grows out of the interplay between social fact and utopian dream. As dialogical structures, usually presented in the form of a dialogue, utopias signal their demand for our participation as readers, a participation that is itself guided by a dialectical logic that sees everything in terms of oppositions and negations. If we open ourselves to these oppositions, then the process of reading utopias can no longer be merely a matter of passively accepting or rejecting the text's formulaic solutions; rather, reading utopias can now become an occasion for a more productive interrogation of social contradictions, an occasion for self-discovery and for making discoveries about the social world in which we live.

To see how utopian texts enfold the reader in a dialogical process that is provocative and productive, let us briefly consider More's exemplary text. The ambivalence that we experience in reading literary utopias—the doubt, skepticism, and disbelief that utopias inspire in us—originates to a great extent in the ambiguous and contradictory status of "Utopia" as a "good-place" (*eu-topia*) that is "no-place" (*ou-topia*). Thomas More drew this double meaning into the name of his famous island and this doubleness has haunted the idea of utopia ever since. For More, this twofold meaning indicated that the society he mapped out in his book is both a good-place and a no-place, a society better than the historical England of his time and a society that exists nowhere in space and time. The resulting ambiguity, however, has engendered disagreements about his intentions that have continued to the present day. Readers still ask what More advocated in his book and wonder how seriously to take what he may have advocated. Is More's work primarily a game, an exercise in wit and playful irony, a literary joke? Or is it serious beneath its playfulness? Is it a revolutionary book that seeks to change a corrupt social system? Or is it a conservative book that longs nostalgically for a simpler time and place? Looked at yet another way, is it merely an escapist book that proposes no specific ideology, offering us but a moment of respite from harsh reality?[2] The basic indeterminacy of More's good-place/no-place has created opposition between readers who stress the attainability of More's good-place and those who stress the irony of the fact that More's good society is nowhere.

But More not only provides us with a description of a fictive island that is at the same time a good-place and a no-place. For alongside this ambivalent "other" place, More also evokes a much more familiar place, an island that is considerably less ambiguous and less happy: historical England of 1516. Thus, as Louis Marin has observed, More's *Utopia* actually maps out two distinct and yet interdependent communities: an imaginary one described in Book II as "the best state of a commonwealth," and a historical one delineated in Book I which, by comparison, is "the worst state of a commonwealth."[3] The most characteristic feature of all utopias is precisely this dialectical structuring that juxtaposes two separate but mutually informing communities representing opposing and contradictory views on social life and social relations. These two communities may be explicitly represented in the text, as they are in More's *Utopia,* or one may be left implicit, as in Plato's *Republic.* In either case, as Marin points out, literary utopias can be identified by two distinct levels of discourse: exposition and critical analysis of social fact, and projection of an imaginary fiction. This twofold activity involves both the defamiliarization of a historical or real time and place—marred by disparities, waste, exploitation, repression—and the invention of an imaginary no-place or no-time in which these contradictions are cancelled or at least reduced. In reading literary utopias, we constantly engage in a process of comparing and contrasting two similar but incompatible images of social life. The potential effects of this process on readers are determined to a large extent by our performance as readers—that is, by the relationship we establish between the utopian dream and the historical reality it tries to transform and displace. To ensure that this process of comparison takes place, utopias usually provide us with a guide who explains the marvelous transformations in utopia to a startled visitor who represents the author's society.

Given the contradictory nature of utopia as a good-place that is no-place and its radical discontinuity with and yet mutual dependence on the historical world of its composition, it is not surprising that readers with different priorities and different ideological perspectives have read and evaluated utopian literature in fundamentally different ways. Nor is it surprising, given the great variety of texts that make up the genre of utopian discourse, that these readers represent different disciplines and diverse interests. As constructs of the imagination, utopias may share a similar method (the projection of alternative social possibilities based on existing relationships) and reach similar conclusions (usually a form of socialism or communal ownership of wealth), but they also differ fundamentally in form, content, and intention. Some utopias are fictive and playful explorations of social possibilities; others are grave and serious proposals intended for immediate implementation. Some are located in another time, others in another place. Some set out to do away with all forms of structure and organization, while others make these elements indispensable features of their design. Some advocate revolutionary change while others are satisfied with gradual reform. Some are constructed on the principles of austerity and discipline, others on the assumption of plenitude and the values of luxury and sensual pleasure. Some, like More's *Utopia*, emphasize the importance of family, monogamy, and religion, while others, like Plato's *Republic*, stress the elimination of all three. There is not even complete agreement on the question of private property: some see it as the origin of all social evil, others see it as necessary to sustain human initiative and progress, still others encourage it on a limited scale, subordinate to solidarity and shared enterprise. Even a cursory glance at the vast array of utopian writings indicates that the works we classify as utopian literature differ in almost every way imaginable. Beyond a general desire for human happiness, justice, and social harmony, utopian literature provides us with a variety of visions that reflect the diverse and contradictory dreams of those who construct them.

Confronted with such a diverse array of texts, readers have approached utopian discourse on different levels and have emphasized different meanings and functions. Some have stressed the political function of these texts and have focused on the utopian method as a critical tool that gives us access to alternative social forms. Some have argued that utopian projections can help us to anticipate and even predict future developments. Others have insisted that all utopian efforts are self-indulgent fantasies, far too abstract and idealistic to have significant impact on social reality. Still others have claimed that utopian visions are pernicious in effect because they direct our attention away from more practical social concerns. Literary critics have focused their analyses on the unique literary properties of utopias, emphasizing their function as an imaginative form of literature and drawing up elaborate ge-

9

neric boundaries to distinguish utopian works from such generic neighbors as myths, the pastoral, the folktale, and the anti-utopia.

In short, different kinds of readers, from disciplines as varied as political science, history, anthropology, psychology, philosophy, futurology, and literary criticism, have read the same texts in different and even contradictory ways. In spite of their differences, we may begin here by dividing these readers into two general groupings: first, those readers whose interests are primarily in the sociopolitical function of these texts, who tend to read all utopias as proposals for social reform and to emphasize their rational (or irrational), constructive (or destructive) features; and second, those readers whose interests are primarily in literature and who tend to read utopias first and foremost as fictions, as products of the imagination that may or may not be intended for realization. Leszek Kolakowski evokes the basic distinction between these approaches when he observes that although "utopia always remains a phenomenon of the world of thought," it is also "a tool of action upon reality and of planning social activity."[4] For both groups of readers, however, utopian works are generally understood as representations of perfect social arrangements that have unambiguous ideological functions: whether purely fictive or intended for realization, they represent ideal forms of social relations and seek to convert the reader to embrace utopian values.

These bifurcated readings of utopian literature have contributed, I would argue, to the generally low regard in which the genre is held. For if, on the one hand, we approach utopias as blueprints for social action, we find that most existing models are reductive, vague, and constraining. Few readers, even sympathetic ones, have been willing to admit that they would like to live in any of these models, assuming it were possible to do so.[5] H. G. Wells observed in his *Modern Utopia* that "there must always be a certain effect of hardness and thinness about utopian speculations," and readers have generally agreed.[6] Marx and Engels, as we shall see in chapter 4, based their polemical attacks on the "utopian socialists" on the abstractness of most utopian proposals, arguing that utopias fail to provide a convincing method for their enactment and are therefore ineffectual in achieving any concrete results.[7] Indeed, even the more concrete models of utopia seem to bear out the *Oxford English Dictionary* definition of utopia as "an impossibly ideal scheme." In most cases, utopian proposals are simply too hazy and too impractical to warrant any serious attempt at realization. Some readers have even argued explicitly that utopian ideals are inevitably deformed— and, indeed, can become monstrous—in the effort to realize them.[8]

If, on the other hand, we approach utopias as works of fantasy and imagination, we cannot help but be disappointed by what we find. For most readers, the basic texts of the genre are stereotypical and uninspiring. On the formal level, they combine political theory, moral philosophy, and sociological analysis for blatantly didactic purposes; on the level of content, they are identified by characteristically long-winded expositions of utopian manners, laws, customs, and institutions. Instead of an ambivalent and provocative no-place, readers find more often that utopia is a boring-place that sets out systematically to eliminate all doubt, conflict, drama, and complexity—the very qualities, in other words, that usually make the experience of reading fiction an exciting and rewarding one.

Existing studies of utopian literature and utopian thought in general have emphasized either its social function, as a critical tool for social action, or its function as literature. Ian Todd and Michael Wheeler, for example, have provided a richly illustrated history of utopian ideals based on the assumption that utopias represent "the perfect society visualized by the world's greatest utopian writers, painters, poets, and architects."[9] Similarly, in his study of English utopias, Richard Gerber defines the texts he analyzes as "skillful descriptions of ideal societies meant to be taken as practical contributions to social reform."[10] For Frank and Fritzie Manuel, the great variety and diversity of utopian discourse can be reduced to the unambiguous function of trying to realize here and now the timeless myth of a perfect paradise.[11]

What this approach to the study of utopias tends to overlook is the apparent paradox that what is rendered as a utopian ideal is by definition "nowhere"; that is, it is merely conceivable or imaginary, not anything actual or necessarily intended for actualization, even if it is presented as such. Moreover, this approach fails to take into account the numerous contradictions concealed behind the apparent realism of the utopian representation, contradictions that become more evident when we consider the conflicting demands that utopian narrative makes on us as readers. For in presenting us with two distinct images of social life, utopias tend to obscure the distance between them and to suppress the essential fact/fiction difference. They do so by averring that the fictive no-place is an actual place existing here and now, on the other side of a mountain, beyond the sea, or in a fully realized future. In thus blurring the distinction between fact and fiction or between history and utopia, utopian texts produce a curious tension in the reader's mind: on the one hand, they suggest that the boundary between fact and fiction is arbitrary, that utopian proposals are "real" or intended for realization; on the other hand, utopian texts also enhance the reader's sense of the distance separating social fact from utopian fiction, a distance that is already indicated by those exclusive boundaries that set utopia off as a remarkable "other-time" or "other-place" radically discontinuous from what is known and real. Our sense of this distance is increased when we recall that utopia is by definition "nowhere," an imaginary projection that is different from and incommensurate with the social reality it transforms.

In thus both sharpening and obscuring the reader's perception of the distance between social fact and utopian fiction, utopian texts make the kinds of demands on readers that are more characteristic of modernist fiction, demands that challenge the reader and require her active participation and intervention in producing the meaning of the text. Modernist forms of literature are, of course, characterized by a readiness to unmask themselves, calling attention to their artificiality and their conventions and thus revealing to the reader the sources upon which their structures of order are based. In general, these texts tend to throw all elements of established order— political, social, moral, aesthetic—into doubt, a doubt from which only the reader can retrieve them. These texts therefore require a higher level of participation from the reader, a level of participation that forces the reader to construct whatever meaning may emerge in the act of reading—a meaning, furthermore, that will always be limited, relative, and doubtful.

Literary utopias, of course, are not so ready to reveal their contingent and artificial status and, indeed, actually try to mask their true nature as fictive no-places. But the effect of this masking, when read dialectically, is also to reveal the nature of any established system as arbitrary, contingent, and provisional. For in exposing existing social forms as arbitrary, utopias have the salutary effect of reminding us that all forms of social organization are provisional and capable of being changed. In terms of their effects on readers, then, utopias, like many modern texts, function to increase our awareness of the historicity of all values and of their human origin. The danger in reading utopias as blueprints for social action is that we forget utopia's fictive status and see it solely as a program for realization. The consequences of such a misreading, as we shall see later, have been vividly depicted in the many anti-

13

utopias that represent what life would be like in a fully realized utopia.

Our tendency to read utopias as proposals for social reform is reinforced by our tendency to identify with the visitor or traveler to utopia, who, like the reader, is a representative of pre-utopian values and finds herself suddenly transported into a strange land, a fully established utopian society. Because the basic situation of this figure in the text parallels the basic situation of the reader, the obvious identification of the two suggests itself as the way in which the utopian author tries to control the reception of the text and to assure that the reader will draw the "correct" conclusions.[12] In this passive model of the reader/text relationship, the reader's task is essentially to listen to the guide's account of life within the boundaries of utopia and, in the end, to recognize the clear superiority of utopian values. This close identification of the reader with the visitor, however, works to limit and constrain the reader's own activity, leaving her in a passive posture in which the options are either to accept or reject the utopian way of life. These passive responses, as we shall see in chapter 3, are ultimately unsatisfactory because they do not account for the problematic position of the reader, suspended between social fact and utopian dream, nor for the potentially unsettling and activating effects that utopias produce in the act of reading.

Reading literary utopias as sociological blueprints that formulate more or less perfect forms of social arrangements may be a way to document the history of utopian ideals, but it does not explain how these texts function as literature. Thus, other readers, mainly literary theorists and critics, have argued that utopias should be read not as proposals for social reform but as forms of imaginative fiction. In his essay "Varieties of Literary Utopias," Northrop Frye has suggested that "utopian thought is imaginative, with its roots in literature, and the literary imagination is less concerned with achieving ends than with visualizing possibilities."[13] This may seem obvious enough, but in view of our tendency to read utopias as documents that formulate social reforms, Frye's observation constitutes an important reminder that utopias are, first of all, fictive constructions. As such, they combine formal structures, generic conventions, and narrative strategies in order to produce certain effects on readers. It becomes important, then, to distinguish more carefully between fictional utopias and nonfictional ones, since this distinction implies different effects in the act of reading and different criteria for evaluation.

In spite of a basic general agreement on the nature of utopian literature, however, this group of readers has not achieved anything like a consensus in determining the value, functions, and effects of literary utopias. Instead, these readers, like those whose interests are in the practical application of utopian proposals, relate utopias to their own frameworks of value and invest them with intentions that reflect their own literary—and extraliterary—priorities. We can distinguish, however, three principal ways in which this second group of readers has determined the functions of literary utopias and inferred their meanings. What identifies each one is a particular emphasis on certain effects that these texts are presumed to have on readers.

There are, first of all, a significant number of literary and social theorists who have maintained that the most important effect of literary utopias is cognitive in nature. For these theorists, utopias are essentially heuristic models of social justice and reason that function to defamiliarize and thereby illuminate existing standards, values, and norms. Darko Suvin's major contribution to the study of utopian literature, as we shall see in the next chapter, is his analysis of utopias in terms of their critical impact, what he calls "cognitive estrangement." For Suvin, the critical force of literary utopias lies in their capacity to distance or "make strange" existing social relations— a technique that is intended to bring the reader to certain recognitions about the nature of social life and social change.

15

This "estrangement effect," according to Suvin, defamiliar-izes existing values, exposes false myths, and generally en-lightens the reader by clarifying what is confused or masked by the prevailing ideology. The question, of course, is whether utopias work solely or even primarily on the basis of such heightened critical reflection. We have already seen that uto-pias set out not only to illuminate existing social relations but also to formulate specific solutions for the reader—solutions, moreover, that require a suspension of our critical faculties along with our disbelief so that we may entertain utopian val-ues. Thus, although I am in essential agreement with Suvin's approach, I will argue that literary utopias are better under-stood in terms of a twofold function that both defamiliarizes a familiar world and seeks to acquaint the reader with a strange, uncanny, and fantastical world.

A second group of theorists has attributed to utopian liter-ature a therapeutic effect that is similar to the function of myth. These critics emphasize the capacity of literary utopias to me-diate or resolve, on the level of imagination, real cultural and social contradictions. The effect of this mediation is to help the reader to cope more adequately in a complex and contradictory social world. Northrop Frye suggests this function when he writes in the essay cited above that "the desirable society, or utopia proper, is essentially the writer's own society with its unconscious ritual habits transposed into their conscious equivalents" (p. 325). By making our unconscious social behav-ior conscious through mythlike projections of balance and har-mony, utopias have not so much a cognitive effect as a consol-ing one: they provide us with an integrated image of society, an image that mediates all oppositions, disparities, inconsis-tencies. For Frye, this mediating function is evident in the universal utopian desire to balance the rival demands of self/society, freedom/happiness, science/religion, rural life/ city life, and so on. Thus, for these readers, utopias function primarily to synthesize antithetical beliefs and contradictory values—a synthesis that helps to ease our fears and apprehensions about the conflicts and antagonisms that exist in society.

A similar therapeutic effect is at the heart of Alvin Toffler's contention that utopian images of the future can condition us to cultural changes, enabling us gradually to accept rapid social change and thus minimizing "future shock."[14] While this way of reading literary utopias does not discount their cognitive impact, it does stress their conciliatory function—the smoothing out of contradictions into a state of noncontradiction—which produces an effect of rest and passivity in the reader rather than stimulating further activity. Suvin's and Marin's ways of reading utopias can be seen as reversing this effect: rather than constituting comforting myths that eliminate all contradictions, these theorists maintain that utopias are not so much perfect versions of the authors' societies as they are "displaced" versions projected into no-time or no-place, the crucial effect of which is to make more acute our perception of contradictions and the essential incompatibility of social fact and utopian dream.

A third group of theorists has maintained that literary utopias not only give us a glimpse of better social possibilities but actually anticipate, or even predict, future developments. This function seems difficult to justify since, for the most part, utopias have not been very successful in predicting or prophesying future events. Still, futurists like Toffler believe that a concerted effort to understand future developments will enable us to forecast and even shape their general contours, while others, mainly Marxist critics, have claimed a more limited anticipatory function for the utopian imagination. Ernst Bloch, for example, who has provided the most comprehensive analysis of the utopian impulse in his two-volume work *Das Prinzip Hoffnung*, celebrated the utopian principle as "a methodical organ for the New."[15] For Bloch, the critical effect of utopia is similar to that of a symbol. Like a symbol, utopia is fertile, multivalent, resonant; it taps our deepest longings for what is not yet manifest, subtly suggesting the way toward a better future in which we will be truly "at home." In Bloch's view, however, utopia has a restricted predictive power: it anticipates in a very indirect way what cannot be understood on the conscious level, expressing the basic "lack" that we sense in the human condition but cannot grasp directly.

Louis Marin attributes a similar anticipatory effect to literary utopias when he argues that "utopian discourse is the one form of ideological discourse that has an anticipatory value of a theoretical kind: but it is a value which can only appear as such when theory has itself been elaborated, that is to say, subsequent to the emergence of the material conditions for the new productive forces."[16] Like Bloch, Marin invests utopia with "an anticipatory value" that can only suggest, on a preconscious level, a future situation that is not yet conceptualizable—a situation, in other words, that becomes apparent only after the theory that accounts for it has emerged. For Marin, this theory is Marxism, which can explain "scientifically" what utopia can only grasp inarticulately and symbolically. Thus, in Marin's view, utopia becomes obsolete with the advent of Marxism. For with the arrival of Marxism on the historical scene, the inarticulate utopian desire for social harmony and community is replaced by the Marxist concept of the "classless society," the hazy symbolic method for realizing social change is replaced by the Marxist method of class struggle and revolution, and the absent agent for realizing utopian change is made concrete in the Marxist proletariat.

Clearly, then, the kind of qualified anticipatory power that Bloch and Marin attribute to utopian discourse is considerably more subtle and less effective than the conscious power to forecast future developments. Marin's claims tend to reinforce the view that the strength of utopia does not lie in its capacity to predict the shape of things to come. In fact, as we

18

shall see later, Marin's reading of More's *Utopia* reduces the author to a semiconscious instrument of the historical process, barely able to perceive the social changes occurring around him. It is only later, after the theoretical framework of Marxism is available to us, that these subtle traces of a future can be discerned by the text's readers.

Today, however, even these subtle traces of a future in More's text appear dated; they indicate a "future" that is, for present-day readers, a situation in the past. Indeed, the more utopias we read, the more evidence we find that the future cannot be anticipated and that any effort to do so is bound to fall short of actual developments. This suggests that the real interest of literary utopias, their most important value for us as readers, is not in anticipating a possible future but in defamiliarizing a present moment—a moment in the history of the author's own society made more comprehensible and more accessible to our understanding. The real power of utopian literature is in its capacity to reveal that present moment as a moment in history, that is, as a temporal horizon of possibilities that is constantly changing. Rather than providing readers with a window into the future—whether Marxist or capitalist or Socialist—utopian literature produces a more important effect in undermining the reader's complacency and apathy about the existing moment in history and in arousing the kind of doubt and dissatisfaction that nurtures utopian activity in the first place.

This brief survey of the various approaches to reading utopian literature has sought to indicate how readers invest utopias with different functions and how they impose their own ideological and literary interests on them. Like all literary works, utopias can be read from different perspectives and are susceptible to different interpretations. Evaluations of literary utopias differ essentially because readers relate them to their own frameworks of value and because they see differently the relationship between social reality and utopian dream: some see it in terms of critical distancing and mutual illumination; others see the utopian dream as a perfect mediation that balances troublesome social contradictions; still others see an anticipatory value that gives us an important, albeit limited, glimpse into the future. Each of these approaches discloses certain possibilities for reading and emphasizes certain effects of these texts at the same time that it closes off others. Each approach is therefore limiting and enabling at the same time.

But, more importantly perhaps, these diverse readings also suggest that utopian literature is not as programmatic, one-dimensional, and single-minded as it is often assumed to be. What these readings indicate is that utopias can and do invite different responses from readers, and that their significance and value cannot be measured without taking these responses into account. Only so long as we approach literary utopias either as blueprints for practical action or as escapist fantasies can we characterize them as constraining and arid. If we approach them instead as dialectical interrogations of social reality in which social fact is momentarily suspended and displaced by a utopian dream—essentially a kind of intellectual experiment whose function is to illuminate the nature of social reality and social change—then their efficacy is recognized to consist neither in their status as fiction nor in their capacity to promote actual reform. Rather, it is seen to lie in this dialectical structuring itself, in the process that plays imaginatively with social possibility and historical necessity, and in the critical impact of this process on readers. The value of literary utopias, in other words, resides in the uncertainty and dissatisfaction that this process arouses in us concerning the nature of existing social relations and our own relationship to the social world in which we live. Their most important effect is to sensitize us to our own moment in history as a transitory moment and to enable us to recognize the historicity of all social forms. If we focus on the potentially liberating effects of literary utopias, we become more aware of the contradictory nature of all utopian undertakings and of the contradictory nature of social reality itself. These same texts that seem to be so dogmatic in their claims and assumptions can now be recognized as "open" texts in the sense that they position us, as readers, in a liberated relationship to the social arrangements they represent—both as they are and as they ought to be—and thus place us squarely in the center of a dialectical inquiry concerning social fact and social possibility.

To realize these potential effects of literary utopias we need to shift our attention from dogmatic utopian claims and solutions to the dialectical process that produces them. It is helpful, in this regard, to define the "act of reading" in Wolfgang Iser's terms as "a process of re-creative dialectics."[17] Reading, for Iser, is an active reciprocal transaction between reader and text that may produce either a "positive" or a "negative" effect in the reader. If it is "positive," the text will tend to sanction and to shore up the values and beliefs already held by its readers; if it is "negative," the text will challenge and undermine those beliefs, stimulating a desire for change and for alternative possibilities. A literary text, according to Iser, may either affirm or negate the values and norms of its historical epoch or culture. Iser cites medieval courtly romance and socialist realism as examples of the kind of literature that seeks to confirm and reinforce existing values. He prefers those texts characterized by negation because they stimulate and provoke the reader to become more productive and more creative in formulating alternative values.

To a certain extent, Iser's distinction may seem arbitrary since all literature can be seen to challenge the norms and values of its readers at some level. Even the most authoritarian texts can have this effect by forcing us to critically reevaluate our own beliefs in relation to those represented in the text. Umberto Eco has shown how even extremely "closed" texts, constructed on a "poetics of necessity," can

21

yield different readings, depending on the reader's perspective, tastes, inclinations, and on the context in which they are read.[18] In the case of literary utopias, moreover, both a negative and a positive effect can be discerned: utopias are negative in the sense that they seek to undermine existing social arrangements and to subvert existing social values, and they are positive in the sense that they formulate a clear alternative, a negation of the negation, that affirms new values and new forms of social arrangements. Literary utopias, in other words, are both subversive and constructive, both critical and affirmative, both negative and positive. Utopias, as we have seen, defamiliarize contradictions existing in the author's society and then go on to prescribe more or less perfect solutions. If we reject these solutions, we place ourselves in the awkward position of having to defend existing social contradictions (an untenable position since these have already been revealed as severe restrictions of human possibilities); if we accept these solutions, we assume a passive posture, merely assenting to utopian prescriptions and thereby minimizing our own critical involvement.

Both these responses are ultimately unsatisfactory because neither takes into account the disturbing and unsettling effect that utopian dialectic produces in the reader. For no matter whether we are sympathetic or antagonistic to the utopian desire to change society, we remain generally unconvinced by the overly optimistic claims and hopelessly naive assumptions upon which this change is predicated: we question the absoluteness with which utopian claims are made, and we feel uneasy about the static and timeless nature of utopian solutions. We sense, further, that the utopian impulse toward change and renewal is contradicted by solutions that are propounded as permanent and unchanging; we begin to perceive, gradually, the incompatibility of the "real" social contradictions and the utopian dream that seeks to cancel them once and for all. Thus, in our actual experience of reading literary utopias, we become more aware of the contradictions and discrepancies that distinguish social fact and that differentiate and distance it from utopian dream; we become aware of inconsistencies that the dialectical structuring makes more apparent. Unable now simply to convert to the utopian solutions, because they are inadequate and by definition "nowhere" in existence, and unable to affirm the social reality that has been exposed as corrupt and restrictive, the reader is, in a real sense, suspended between two alternatives, neither of which is satisfactory or tenable.

If the reader responds to this inconclusive situation, she must necessarily become more active. Armed with a set of contradictions and a host of questions, and thrown back on her own resources, the reader must engage the terms of the text's dialectic in an inquiry that becomes her own. In actively questioning the formulations provided by the text, the reader participates more fully in a reading that becomes an unfolding of the terms of the dialectic—a dialectic embedded not just in the text but in the social realities with which the text is concerned. Such a reader participates in what Suvin has called "the open or hidden dialogues of utopian texts,"[19] what Michael Holquist has recognized as the essential "gamelike" structures of such texts,[20] and what Marin has analyzed as the essential components of utopian narrative.[21] Such a productive reader is the kind that Ursula K. Le Guin has called for as the appropriate reader for her own "ambiguous utopias" and, by extension, for the texts of the genre as a whole: *the reader as partner.*[22]

The recognition that this is the kind of "model" reader implied by utopian literature constitutes an important shift in focus from the formulaic utopian solutions themselves to the dialogical process of working them out, a shift in emphasis from understanding literary utopias as final products (visions of perfection or blueprints for action) to grasping them as tentative and provisional explorations. This change in focus seems difficult at first, given the characteristic utopian effort to demonstrate the unconditional happiness of utopia's citizens and the perfection of all its institutions—and given the utopian strategy of obscuring the differences between social fact and utopian fantasy. To justify this shift, we will have to consider in chapter 3 the formal and narrative features that allow us to grasp a literary utopia as an informing process rather than as a representational object or a final design. What is important now is that we recognize how our readings and evaluations of utopian literature are determined to a great extent by our own ideological presuppositions and our priorities as readers. If we evaluate literary utopias in terms of their feasibility and practicality, then only a handful will be found viable; if we judge them by the standards of logic, consistency, and coherence, very few will withstand rigorous examination; if we look for drama, excitement, complexity, and conflict, then reading utopias will prove to be a rather disappointing experience. If, however, we focus on the dialectical structuring at the heart of all utopias and entertain the oppositions, tensions, and contradictions that this structuring uncovers, we discover the essential value of these texts, not in any properties in the texts themselves, but in their startling and provocative effects on readers.

This shift will allow us to stress the process of utopian activity itself—a value that is often overlooked in discussions of literary utopias. As Gary Saul Morson has observed concerning Plato's *Republic*, "Much of the interest and reward of reading the *Republic*, even for those who are uninterested in or antagonistic to its politics and philosophy, lies in the *process* by which Socrates recognizes, formulates, works out, and finally solves philosophic problems. The *Republic*, in other words, does not simply offer solutions, but represents the activity of finding them—an activity which, in Plato's rendition, attains considerable dramatic power."[23] Morson refers to the *Republic* as "a work in progress," an appropriate designation,

I think, for the unfinished nature of all utopian efforts and one that suggests a more active role for the reader. Even though few utopias achieve the level of "dramatic power" that Morson finds in Plato's text, all of them (including anti-utopias) can be seen as "works in progress," works that engage the reader in a dynamic process of discovery, a process that intensifies social tensions and contradictions at the same time that it appears to cancel them.

2

Disputed Boundaries
Defining the Utopian Terrain

That which is without boundaries and hence cannot be grasped is, for man, also without meaning. Only by drawing boundaries in the thought-realm can we produce a problem which can be grasped and worked with.

— FRED L. POLAK, *The Image of the Future*

Utopian literature is inherently dialogic in nature and is best understood as an invitation to the reader to enter into a dialectical thought process concerning the nature of social possibility. But since readers, as a rule, constitute such a heterogeneous group, reflecting many conflicting interests, tastes, and priorities, utopian literature has a varied history in which different readers, or different groups of readers, have appropriated it and imbued it with different meanings. The result is that utopia's peaceful and harmonious landscape is also a field for ideological contention and dispute. In this chapter I will survey the kinds of conflicting readings that literary utopias have elicited and show how our comprehension of these texts is always modified by our own ideological perspectives and by our strategies as readers. Since literary utopias set out to question our routine habits of perception and to transform our social beliefs, it is almost impossible to remain neutral concerning their aims and intentions. The experience of reading utopias is essentially an encounter with an unfamiliar or foreign territory whose institutions and social arrangements are designed to startle us, to challenge our social values, and to undermine our assumptions about social reality. Utopian literature, in short, is designed to change us. But just as utopian works seek to modify the reader, they are also modified by him through his performance as a reader. In a dialectical model of the reader/text relationship, neither reader nor text is a stable entity or a finished product; each constitutes, rather, an active component in a mutual transaction that produces discord, disagreement, and transformation.

The origin of many of the disputes and battles waged over the utopian landscape can be traced to the ever-present barriers that enclose it and separate it from the surrounding terrain. Ever since More described his island Utopia, boundaries, walls, trenches, moats, and a variety of other spatial and temporal barriers have been indispensable features on subsequent maps of utopia.[1] The function of these barriers is, of course, to protect what is inside from outside influence and contamination. To this end, they are usually formidable, well-fortified, and made nearly impassable. This exclusiveness seems appropriate enough when we recall that what these boundaries are designed to protect is by definition the best of all possible worlds; any change through outside influence would therefore be automatically a change for the worse. But in protecting the utopian territory, these boundaries also isolate and insulate it, cutting it off from the rest of human society and transforming it into a static place that seems incapable of change, novelty, innovation. Thus, the function of these barriers, like almost everything else about utopia, is twofold: seen from the inside, they function to keep disorder and chaos out; seen from the outside, they function to keep docile and unknowing inhabitants within and can be read as an unambiguous sign of utopia's desire to escape the uncertainties and contingencies of time and history.

But these boundaries may also be understood as a metaphor for the crucial distinction between the imaginary component of the utopian text, or utopia proper, and its "real" or historical component, the social world of its composition. These boundaries, then, function to provide us with an essential vantage point, a perspective which allows us to perceive both the "otherness" of the utopian territory and the historical immediacy of the more familiar territory from which it is set off. Implicitly or explicitly, as we have already seen, utopias evoke two discrete and yet mutually informing pictures of social life: one defamiliarizes the deficiencies that exist in the author's society; the other elaborates a fictive permutation, a static picture that reduces and simplifies the complexity and teeming multiplicity of the author's society. What becomes crucial in our interpretation of utopian literature is the way in which we link these images. This will determine whether we regard utopias as fictions constructed on imaginary permutations of social fact or as more serious guides for social action—or, if we read their boundaries with greater subtlety, as playful and inconclusive intellectual experiments, conducted entirely in the imagination, that test the boundaries of the reader's own imagination.

Different perceptions of these boundaries have played a pivotal role in determining our understanding and evaluation of utopian literature. As we briefly observed above, those readers interested in the pragmatic value of utopian proposals have not differentiated between fictional utopias and other kinds of utopian discourse. For these readers, all utopian texts are essentially discursive documents that detail closed social systems intended for implementation. The boundaries that separate social fact from utopian fiction are, for these readers, pedagogical devices whose significance is that they touch both utopia and the "real" world at the same time and thus represent the conceivability of social harmony within the horizon of the world as we know it.

Among this group of readers we find attitudes ranging from Karl Mannheim's vigorous defense of utopian thinking to Karl Popper's insistence that all utopian efforts are socially harmful, insidious, and self-defeating.[2] What unites this diverse group of readers—whether pro- or anti-utopian—is their interest in utopian thought as a mode of social knowledge and social planning. These readers study a variety of utopian writings as sociological or ideational documents from which they derive pragmatic social propositions. Thus, they tend to favor the more concrete utopian proposals over the more fantastic or fanciful ones. Their approach is general and pluralistic. They regard all utopias as more or less perfect forms of social organization that can be judged in terms of their feasibility, appropriateness, suggestiveness, or, in Mannheim's case, in terms of their critical impact on existing ideology. For this group of readers, utopias are evaluated primarily as a method of social analysis that is both critical of existing social relations and conducive to the production of alternative forms, and they argue for or against this method as a tool for planning social alternatives.

Those who oppose the utopian method of social speculation argue that it is naive, self-indulgent, abstract, and unscientific; proponents, on the other hand, see utopian thinking as inherent in all significant social change and argue that a society without a utopian dimension will eventually stagnate and congeal in one-dimensionality. In *Ideology and Utopia*, for example, Karl Mannheim claimed that without the productive effects of the utopian imagination, we lose not only our ability to shape the world in which we live, but even our ability to comprehend it (p. 263). Similar arguments have been made by Fred L. Polak, who invests utopias with the vital function of going beyond the status quo, an orientation that seeks constantly to transcend the boundaries of the existing order.[3] Others have argued that the atrophying influences of mass culture and mass consumption have made the production of utopian images

29

more urgent than ever before. Futurist Alvin Toffler, for example, has proposed the establishment of "collaborative utopias" in which teams of social scientists, engineers, psychologists, ecologists, fiction writers, and so forth, engage in envisioning productive and pragmatic "images of potential tomorrows."[4] Anthropologist Margaret Mead wrote that "the very survival of the human race and possibly all living creatures depends on having a vision of the future for others which will command our deepest commitment."[5] Political theorist Andrew Hacker has urged that utopian thinking "should be one of the main foundation stones of the body of theory now being created," and he has called upon political scientists to "create their own utopias and commit them to paper."[6] Images of such potential utopias were provided in the 1960s by Herbert Marcuse and Paul Goodman, for whom utopia implied nonrepressive societies giving free play to libidinal freedom and aesthetic imagination.[7]

Despite the otherwise important differences that separate these social thinkers, they can be seen to share a similar attitude toward the functions of utopian literature and thought. They all tend to grasp the idea of utopia as an important diagnostic tool whose efficacy lies in its usefulness in analyzing social problems and projecting possible solutions. For such thinkers, individual utopian texts can therefore be evaluated as detailed representations that envision constructive and creative alternatives to counter the prevailing forces of apathy, conformity, and repression. As efforts to change social relations, these visions are intended to replace the deformed and dehumanized relations that prevail at any given time. The boundaries that for literary specialists indicate the radical fictionality of utopia are generally disregarded in this approach. As representations of political ideals, utopias provide straightforward solutions to social problems—solutions intended to persuade the reader to move toward their realization.

It is precisely from this functional perspective that utopias are most frequently evaluated. A recent example is provided by Goodwin and Taylor's *The Politics of Utopia: A Study in Theory and Practice* (1982), which presents a defense of utopian thought as a method of social analysis that is both critical and constructive. The authors argue for this method on the basis that it counters the predominantly empiricist mode of political thought—with its debilitating demands for feasibility and probability—by projecting more imaginative possibilities. But, while they argue that the strength of the utopian method is in its "counterfactual" or fictive nature—giving greater freedom to the political imagination—they proceed to evaluate utopian proposals on the basis of their practical application and potential for implementation. This is evident in their discussion of numerous utopian communities, both religious and secular, which they consider to have been relatively successful. Although the authors recognize that "the question of whether a utopia is fictional or directly didactic . . . may in turn have repercussions on its effectiveness," they also state that "this distinction is not of great importance . . . since political propositions have successfully been conveyed in utopias of many forms."[8] This emphasis on the propositions themselves and the general reluctance to distinguish between fictional and nonfictional components of utopias is typical of this approach.

A similar orientation can be seen in Frank and Fritzie Manuel's ambitious work *Utopian Thought in the Western World* (1979).[9] This impressively detailed and informative study sets out to provide "a true history of Utopian Thinking" in the tradition exemplified by Lewis Mumford's pioneering work *The Story of Utopias* (1922) and by Todd and Wheeler's richly illustrated *Utopia* (1978). Interested primarily in the history of utopian ideas, these studies are general and "ecumenical" in their method. The Manuels, for example, analyze diverse "utopian" writing and discuss such disparate thinkers as More, Leibniz, Kant, Marx, Hobbes, Herbert Marcuse, Norman O. Brown, and Paolo Soleri. Implicit in their understanding of the "broad universe of utopian discourse" is the assumption that utopias are straightforward representations of political ideals which give us access to a specific historical context and to the author's psychological disposition. Our task in reading utopias is essentially to reconstruct this ideal as the key to the text's meaning—a task made easy by the Manuels' equation of meaning with the utopian author's stated intention.

With these premises, the Manuels trace what they call "a utopian propensity" from ancient to contemporary times. Their goal is to identify the "historical constellations" in which this propensity manifests itself and to trace the "multifarious changes of the utopian experience through the centuries" (p. 5). This method allows the Manuels to convey a sense of the rich diversity of utopian thought, but it also reveals some of the problems inherent in what has come to be called "utopology." These problems result from the Manuels' "latitudinarian and ecumenical conception of Utopia" (p. 7) and from their reluctance to make distinctions among the kinds of utopian texts they are studying.

Recognizing the diversity of utopian discourse and the plurality of meanings associated with utopia, the Manuels nevertheless insist that "an excess of clarity and definition" would only result in "polluting utopia's natural environment" (p. 5). The only definition they are willing to provide is that of utopia as a "myth of heaven on earth" (p. 7), a definition that abruptly dismisses the kinds of distinctions often made between static and dynamic utopias, individual and collective utopias, and classical and libidinal utopias, as well as the distinction between ideology and utopia. Like Goodwin and Taylor, the Manuels acknowledge that some utopias are "dramatic narrative portrayals" while others are discursive tracts, treatises for reform, and blueprints for enactment. But they argue that distinctions here are futile because "the descriptive and discursive rhetorical modes in Utopia are never, or rarely ever, found in a simon-pure state" (p. 4) and because "the line between a utopian system and political and social theory" is usually blurred. While this is indeed the textual strategy of most utopias, the critical refusal to draw any boundaries in the vast utopian terrain leads to vague generalities. In failing to distinguish between the function of "sociopolitical analysis" and the function of "utopian fiction," the Manuels are unable to take into account the consequences that this distinction entails and the different effects it may produce in readers. Instead, the Manuels bring together a great variety of texts under the label "utopian discourse" and read them as historical documents that render ideal societies, perfect states, and idealized forms of social relations. These social ideals are then interpreted as indices of the author's historical environment and of the author's psychology. Indeed, identity-psychology is of primary interest to the Manuels. Thus, for example, More's *Utopia* is found to reveal the author's deep-seated melancholy and his obsession with death and penance, and Babeuf's revolutionary fervor is traced to his rebellion against his father. Certainly, this approach represents a legitimate area for investigation, but the Manuels' emphasis on psychological interpretation tends to reduce the rich variety of utopian discourse to the expression of an assortment of individual aberrations and forms of compensation.

In general, the Manuels' analysis of utopian literature is marred by their failure to provide a conceptual framework and by a more general failure to define their object of study. This results in a rather casual approach that proceeds from one historical epoch to the next, or from one theme to the next, stopping here and there, at more or less arbitrary points, to comment on the "utopian configurations" they find. Essentially, their study constitutes a series of portraits of famous utopian thinkers who, in the estimate of the Manuels, deserve special recognition. The utopian works themselves are useful insofar as they reveal the psychological condition of these thinkers.

What such studies of utopian literature tend to ignore are the potentially activating and liberating effects that utopias can have as forms of narrative fiction. This is understandable since what seems most vital about utopian texts are the political and social issues they take up. Moreover, it is precisely as fiction that utopias have proved so deeply disappointing to most readers. As we observed earlier, utopias are generally considered to lack irony, humor, psychological complexity, drama—elements which, for most readers, constitute the primary interests in reading fiction. Readers are also quick to note the apparent failure of most literary utopias to envision a fictive alternative that is truly "other," new, or radically different. Overall, the fictive worlds described in these texts seem all-too-familiar, predictable, and redundant. Those who advocate a revival of the utopian imagination have recognized this limitation and have urged utopian writers to provide "more vivid" and more inspiring images—images which, in the words of Margaret Mead, are "not too immediate . . . and not too distant," but "complex . . . enough to catch and hold the imaginations of men and women" (p. 959).

Meanwhile, however, literary scholars are confronted with the problem of justifying a group of texts generally considered to lack literary merit. The task is complicated by the fact that literary utopias tend to be such "impure" works, combining heterogeneous materials and different modes of discourse. Robert Elliot has observed that "fictional utopia is a bastard form, answering the claims of a number of disciplines."[10] Nevertheless, literary specialists generally agree that utopias are structured as forms of imaginative fiction and that failure to take this into account can lead to misunderstandings in determining their functions and effects. "To design a text as literature," Gary Saul Morson points out, "is to make a statement about how its meaning is and is not to be determined, about what procedures for deriving propositional value are appropriate. Even if one's primary interest is in the history of ideas rather than literature, it is necessary to know whether a text *is* literature, and if so, what semiotic consequences its literariness entails, in order to interpret it according to its original design."[11] Distinct from the ecumenical and casual approach represented by the Manuels, literary theorists are more concerned with defining the utopian terrain and distinguishing its boundaries. They aspire to a more systematic approach to the study of utopia by providing a theoretical framework that delimits its formal and generic features.

Yet, while literary specialists agree on the principle of making generic and formal distinctions in order to specify the proper use of these texts, they are not in agreement on where these boundary lines should be drawn. In practice, different literary and ideological commitments lead to different typologies and definitions. Thus, numerous boundaries have been drawn and redrawn within the vast utopian landscape—boundaries that distinguish static or machinelike utopias from dynamic or organic ones, spiritual from sensual models, abstract visions from concrete blueprints, individualist from collectivist models, fictional utopias from nonfictional ones. The territory claimed shifts from one attempt to the next; the distinctions carefully drawn up by one classifier are discarded by the next. We should be aware of the limitations of these efforts at generic classification at the same time that we recognize them as important steps in determining how the meanings and potential effects of literary utopias can be realized.

An examination of two exemplary systems will serve to illustrate both the benefits and the shortcomings of this approach to literary utopias. The first is Darko Suvin's effort in his important essay "Defining the Literary Genre of Utopia";[12] the second is Gary Saul Morson's *Boundaries of Genre*. Suvin's essay, taking as its starting point the literary typology of Northrop Frye,[13] defines the genre on the basis of "cognitive estrangement," a dramatic technique that defamiliarizes a familiar world. Morson's formalist-semiotic approach identifies literary utopias as heterogeneous works which combine fiction and nonfiction and constitute a special category, "boundary works," whose meanings depend largely on the conventions according to which they are read. Both Suvin's and Morson's approaches are useful for the insights they offer into the working of utopian texts; that is, both approaches help to determine the kinds of effects that literary utopias have, or are intended to have, on readers. Neither, however, provides a system that is completely satisfactory.

Suvin's effort to define the boundaries of literary utopias blends, in his words, "a warm Marxist attention to historical specificity with a Formalist attention to material forms of textuality" (p. x). But since utopia is situated on a shifting historical terrain and since it is a hybrid form (partaking of the characteristics of various forms), he acknowledges that generic definitions of utopia cannot be firm and permanent. His aim, therefore, is to provide a "heuristic model" that yields practical understanding, not to erect sharp and definitive borders. For Suvin, literary genres are "socioaesthetic and not metaphysical entities," and as such they are "contextualist" rather than "essentialist," providing a general framework for pragmatic understanding (p. 16).

With these premises, Suvin proposes a central distinction between "naturalistic genres" and "estranged genres." The former, he suggests, set out "faithfully to reproduce empirical gestures, surfaces, and relationships vouched by human senses and common sense"; the latter seek "to illuminate men's relationships to other men and to their surroundings

36

by the basic device of a radically different location for the postulated novel human relations of [the work's] fable" (p. 53). What Suvin detects in the "estranged genres," in other words, is the principle of estrangement or defamiliarization. These genres, among which Suvin includes science fiction, utopian fiction, myth, fantasy, the folktale, and the pastoral, do not merely reflect or mirror the world of their composition but rather deflect or refract it in such a way as to make it appear "strange." Suvin defines the function and effect of estrangement by quoting Ernst Bloch: "The real function of estrangement is—and must be—the provision of a shocking mirror above an all too familiar reality" (p. 54).

The "shocking mirror" presented by utopian works creates, according to Suvin, a particularly "cognitive" effect: utopias defamiliarize the author's sociohistorical environment in order to expose its flaws and contradictions and make them transparent to critical understanding. "Cognitive estrangement" constitutes for Suvin the identifying response to the utopian landscape (and, as we shall see, to the terrains depicted in science fiction, dystopian fiction, and certain other kinds of works). It sets utopia apart from generic neighbors such as myth, which limits cognition because it views human relations as fixed and supernaturally determined, and the folktale and fantasy, which are "indifferent to cognition" and deal with supernatural themes. While such estranged forms as the pastoral and the legends of Cockayne and the Earthly Paradise are nearer to utopia in focusing on this-worldly happiness, they are excluded from the utopian terrain either because they are "pure wishdreams" (p. 57) or because they fail to emphasize "sociopolitical institutions and norms as a key to eliminating misery, sickness, injustice" (p. 58). Suvin concludes that "if Cockayne is the land for sensuality, Earthly Paradise for heroes, and pastoral for swains (shepherds as philosophers, poets, and lovers), utopia is the land for natu-

37

ralistic human figures just slightly larger (more virtuous) than everyday nature" (pp. 58–59). Suvin's carefully worded definition is as follows:

> Utopia is a verbal construction of a particular quasi-human community where sociopolitical institutions, norms, and individual relationships are organized according to a more perfect principle than in the author's community, this construction being based on estrangement arising out of an alternative historical hypothesis. (p. 49)

As the emphasis on "quasi-human community" suggests, Suvin's interest in utopian literature coincides with his interest in science fiction. This is apparent in his assertion that "utopia is not a genre but a sociopolitical subgenre of science fiction" (p. 61). Science fiction, a kind of metagenre, embraces a much larger territory which, in Suvin's view, includes not only utopian fiction but also dystopian fiction, "planetary novels," *Staatsromane*, "anticipation novels"—in short, all those forms in which he detects the principle of "cognitive estrangement." What is left outside this not very exclusive territory are naturalistic novels and those estranged forms that are unhistorical and/or noncognitive (such as myth and fantasy). Thus, the mimetic and noncognitive forms become, in Suvin's ideological system, a kind of straw man against which the virtues of the estranged forms can be set off.

One can argue with certain aspects of Suvin's system. His own interests and priorities are evident, for example, in his definition of "naturalistic genres" as mimetic forms that merely record "gestures, surfaces, and relationships." But surely even the most extreme kinds of naturalism seek to accomplish more than a mere replication of the surfaces of the author's time and place. Further, the boundaries that Suvin draws around utopian literature and science fiction are almost identical (not surprisingly, he concludes that "SF can only be written between the utopian and the anti-utopian horizon"

38

[pp. 61–62]). In extending the boundaries of utopia to include science fiction, Suvin is attempting to gain greater recognition and acceptance of the latter by associating it more closely with the utopian tradition. This is somewhat ironic since utopian literature is itself not highly regarded as literature, although it apparently has achieved greater recognition and regard than the science fiction texts Suvin is seeking to justify.

These are minor objections if we recall that Suvin's opposition of naturalistic and estranged genres is not intended to distinguish between fixed essences but rather to indicate an underlying attitude and a shift in emphasis. "Cognitive estrangement" does indeed describe what is potentially the most significant effect of utopian literature—its capacity to disturb and unsettle its readers, to provoke critical thought through the projection of alternate forms of social arrangements. (I qualify this effect as a potential one because these texts will not, of course, have this effect for an inactive or a passive reader.) Utopias do, however, present a dimension that is not fully accounted for by the concept of cognitive estrangement, for they not only defamiliarize or "make strange" a deformed social situation but also seek to familiarize a clear alternative—a fictive "other" situation in which all forms of estrangement have been overcome. Utopias, in other words, not only defamiliarize "what is" but also formulate answers in terms of "what ought to be." Thus, as Suvin himself observes, literary utopias are "positive negations" (p. 54); that is, utopias make us aware of the distance between the "is" and the "ought," allowing for critical reflection and cognition, and at the same time they diminish the importance of this distance, urging us to convert to the wisdom and truth represented by the utopian transformation. Although these two operations are implied in the concept of estrangement, they are not fully distinguished by Suvin as separate strategies: criticism of social fact *and* projection of utopian fantasy. The former is negative, critical, cognitive; the latter is affirmative, suspends critical faculties, and inhibits cognition by blurring the very boundaries between fact and fiction.

Ultimately, Suvin's definition of utopia as "a verbal construction" makes it clear that he sees utopias as forms of literature. Nevertheless, he also recognizes that often the distinction between fictional and nonfictional utopias "is a historically fugitive one" (p. 59). As utopian texts free themselves from their historical environment, it becomes increasingly difficult to tell which were intended as fiction and which were intended for realization or even partial implementation. Suvin acknowledges that "the same text can have opposite meanings" (p. 59), but he is reluctant to face the consequences that this recognition implies. For if a text can be read in opposing ways, then efforts to draw up generic boundaries become problematic indeed. We may decide, then, like the Manuels, to reject efforts at generic description altogether on the grounds that this is a hopeless task and focus instead on a vague "utopian propensity." For Suvin, utopias are neither blueprints for realization nor by definition beyond all attempts at realization (once realized, however, they would cease to be utopian). Instead, Suvin locates the critical impact of utopias in their method, which he compares to Vaihinger's "as if"—a kind of intellectual experiment conducted in the imagination in the subjunctive mood. Suvin finds that, understood this way, utopia is a "method rather than a state, it cannot be realized or not realized—it can only be applied" (p. 52). In its application, utopia becomes, like Suvin's generic definition, a "heuristic device" that helps us to recognize and understand existing forms of alienation and injustice.

But to apply a method that is derived from a literary text means, first of all, that we read the text—an activity that takes place between reader and text. And this dialectical transaction is determined by the interpretative operations of readers as well as by strategies embedded in the text. We have seen that readers like the Manuels refuse to make formal and generic distinctions and read utopias as documents that reflect the psychological states of their authors and mirror specific historical environments. The Manuels thereby suspend the conventions of reading utopias as "verbal constructions based on estrangement" and read them instead with conventions derived from those naturalistic genres from which Suvin painstakingly sets them apart. Among the other reasons we have indicated, the boundaries around utopia are disputed because different readers with different priorities, values, and ideological commitments continue to read utopias in fundamentally different ways.

Recognizing that "genre does not belong to texts alone, but to the interaction between texts and a classifier," Gary Saul Morson has contended that "interpretive conventions rather than formal features determine a work's genre" (p. viii). This shift in focus from formal properties in the text to the "interpretive conventions" of readers has some important implications for determining the potential effects of literary utopias. First, it suggests that the meaning of a literary text is a function of the conventions according to which it is read; literary utopias, therefore, are not simply documents from which a single meaning can be drawn but will yield different meanings depending on the conventions applied in the act of reading. Second, this shift redirects our attention from the formal and semantic features in the text to the more complex interrelationship between reader and text.

Morson begins his study by observing that literary utopias are "taxonomically ambiguous" works, similar to such marginal literary forms as the autobiography, the diary, the fragment, and the preface. These "boundary works," as Morson refers to them, can be identified by the heterogeneous and incompatible materials that make up their contents: narrative, essay, travel reports, fantasy, social satire, sketches, and so forth. In combining various forms, these hybrid works are comparable, in Morson's analogy, to a territory to which two or more sides lay claim, or to a person with dual citizenship. Because they combine diverse materials, these forms are ambivalent: their contents can be mapped out in different ways, their boundaries can be drawn along different lines.

Rather than constituting a shortcoming, however, this admixture of materials can be seen as the most productive feature of these texts. In Morson's view, such "boundary works" are "designed to resonate between opposing genres and interpretations" (p. 182). The loss of generic assurance that we experience in reading these texts leaves us suspended between two or more possible interpretations, thereby increasing their "resonance" and their potential effects. Morson points out, for example, how our reading of More's *Utopia* will vary depending on the generic conventions we apply. If we read it with the conventions derived from Erasmus's *Praise of Folly* (often considered a companion text), we will tend to interpret *Utopia* as an ironic, playful, and inconclusive dialogue; if, on the other hand, we read it within the tradition and conventions derived from programmatic utopias like Campanella's *City of the Sun* or Bellamy's *Looking Backward*, we will tend to conclude that *Utopia* is a serious proposal for social action and reform. Both readings are possible and both can be persuasive. Rather than insisting that one or the other is correct, it seems more sensible to admit that More's "impure" and ambiguous text can yield different meanings depending on the interpretative conventions we apply. In acknowledging both possibilities, we recognize More's text as a "boundary work" that "exploits the resonance between two kinds of reading" (p. 50).

What is appealing about Morson's concept of "boundary works" is that it seems to rescue literary utopias from their one-dimensional status as either reductive arguments for socialism or escapist fantasies. As ambiguous "boundary works," utopias are able to generate some complexity and ambiguity in the act of reading—they become multifaceted texts whose significance depends in part on how we read them. However, when Morson goes on to draw up his own boundaries, he classifies literary utopias on the basis of their "semiotic nature," by which he means "the conventions that govern, or are assumed to govern, how the meanings of such texts are to be inferred" (p. 74). Since, in Morson's view, literary meaning is solely a function of the generic conventions according to which we read a text, his own classification reflects currently dominant conventions. In other words, Morson emphasizes reading conventions to such an extent that he pushes both the individual reader and the text into the background and describes the effects of literary utopias in terms of current conventions. When other conventions become operative, then presumably the range and potential significance of literary utopias will also change. In the meantime, however, Morson's description of the utopian terrain is based upon existing notions about utopian literature and existing attitudes toward it and thus tends to reinscribe the constraints most often placed upon it.

In mapping out the contours of the literary utopia, Morson provides three criteria to distinguish it from the nonliterary utopia, the anti-utopia, and other fantastic narratives. These criteria are: (1) literary utopias are "written (or presumed to have been written) in the tradition of previous utopian literary works"; (2) utopia "depicts (or is taken to depict) an ideal society"; (3) utopia "advocates (or is taken to advocate) the realization of that society" (p. 74). Since these criteria reflect widely held views on literary utopias, I will consider each in some detail.

Morson's first criterion follows from his premise that literary meaning is a function of generic conventions. For Morson, literary utopias (like all texts) are purely relational entities whose meanings depend on their intertextual relations with other texts that they may cite, rework, parody, or transform in other ways. Thus, Morson concludes, "the original text is in effect re-created by its progeny" (p. 75). Such "exemplary texts" of the genre as More's *Utopia* and Plato's *Republic* achieve this status retrospectively, that is, through subsequent texts that, as Morson puts it, they have "fathered." These subsequent works establish the tradition and genre of the literary utopia by providing the conventions according to which the earlier works are read and from which they receive their significance. In Morson's view, this criterion is valid for all genres, setting up a "generic contract" between author and reader that ensures the proper reception of a work. It is only by "generic re-creation," that is, by reading the work in terms of different generic conventions, that potentially new meanings can emerge.

This emphasis on generic conventions accounts for the way in which utopias are often read, but it can't account for our ability to interpret the first utopian text we encounter (or, indeed, the first example of any genre we encounter). Thus, while it explains how genres come about, it doesn't fully account for the actual transaction between reader and text. More important, it limits considerably the potential responses that a reader can make to a text. Since, for Morson, the significance we derive from literary utopias is determined primarily by generic conventions, both reader and text seem to play minimal roles in the act of interpretation. Readers remain passively subject to existing conventions rather than actively engaging and responding to individual texts. Any potentially new readings are dependent on the application of still other conventions that allow or enable the reader to see different facets of the work. But such an application can only be made, after all, by a reader. The problem with Morson's approach, it seems to me, is that it does not finally recognize that it is individual readers who create the critical practice that creates genres. A text, or a genre, is read one way until readers decide to try to read it another way. Morson's conception of "boundary works" is itself a good example of how this can happen. Applying this conception to literary utopias, he shows how these texts invite and reward various kinds of interpretation, but he limits the potential of this recognition to the existing conventions that shape and determine each individual reading.

Morson's second requirement—that utopia "depicts (or is taken to depict) an ideal society"—is meant to distinguish literary utopias from literary anti-utopias. This distinction becomes problematical in view of the effects that even the "exemplars of the genre" have had on subsequent readers. Very few readers, for example, even sympathetic ones, have found that More's *Utopia* or Plato's *Republic* depict ideal forms of social organization. In fact, most modern readers, conditioned by the values of freedom, innovation, and self-expression, have seen these societies as authoritarian, repressive, even life-denying. Plato's intention may have been "to secure the greatest possible happiness for the community as a whole,"[14] and More's intention may have been to describe "the best state of a commonwealth," but as these texts free themselves from their historical context it becomes difficult for them to enforce their authors' original intentions. In other words, what constitutes an ideal society changes as the historical situation changes and as reading conventions change. The fact that one generation's utopia constitutes another generation's anti-utopia clearly reveals the historical nature of all reading and all readings. It becomes important, then, that we historicize our conception of utopias, recognizing that they cannot be understood in reified terms—as static images of timeless ideals—but are more clearly understood as relative projections of better social relations than those prevailing in the author's society. For, as Suvin points out, once we historicize our conception of literary utopias, "we have . . . no further excuse for insisting on absolute perfection, but only on a state radically better or based on a more perfect principle than that prevailing in the author's community" (p. 45). From a historical perspective, in short, the effort to construct firm boundaries around the utopian terrain becomes an impossible task, and this underscores the reader's role in determining the meaning of these texts.

Morson's third criterion—that utopia "advocates (or is taken to advocate) the realization of [the ideal society depicted]"—seeks to distinguish literary utopias from folktales, myths, and legends of a Golden Age. Like the Manuels, Morson notes that "anticipation and planning, not nostalgia and resignation, characterize the mood of literary utopias" (p. 76), and he concludes that the authors of all utopias advocate, implicitly or explicitly, the realization of their ideal society. But, once again, what is intended in a literary text cannot always be readily determined, particularly once the text is removed from its historical context. Can we know with certainty, for example, which parts of More's *Utopia* or of Bellamy's *Looking Backward* were intended for realization and which parts were meant as playful speculation? Moreover, in emphasizing the utopian tendency to advocate concrete programs for social reform and action, Morson seems to abandon his own definition of boundary works, which affect readers in decidedly ambivalent ways. Utopia, after all, is by definition "nowhere"—a constantly receding goal that exists only in the realm of possibility—and utopian writers have for the most part always understood this.

In Morson's description, then, the literary utopia remains a highly determined territory. His generic criteria seem to firmly reestablish the conventional boundaries that have enclosed utopia in a kind of literary ghetto. For Morson, the great majority of utopian texts remain politically programmatic and predictable efforts to induce us to embrace timeless social formulas. In the process they simplify and reduce the complexities and contingencies of history, diminish aesthetic experience, and make categorical claims about morality and social justice. Morson concludes: "Utopia, in short, surveys and describes a world that is not as complex as it has been thought to be, a world where psychology, history, and social problems are a Gordian knot to be immediately cut rather than laboriously untied" (p. 77). As such, literary utopias remain rather simplistic undertakings—"diatribes rather than dialogues"—richly deserving of the low regard in which they are held.

Given this description of utopian literature, it is difficult to see how it corresponds with Morson's category of "boundary works." And, in fact, Morson divides utopian literature into three distinct subgenres—unambiguous utopias, anti-utopias, and meta-utopias. The criteria that Morson uses for generic definition of the literary utopia are apparently derived solely from those unambiguous utopias that he finds to be formulaic and predictable. The genre anti-utopia consists of those works that parody these formulaic and simplified works, while meta-utopias are those works in which "utopia and its parody enter into an inconclusive dialogue" (p. x). In Morson's view, only meta-utopias are capable of producing the kind of ambivalence that can make the experience of reading utopias "resonant," "unsettling," and "hermeneutically perplexing." Morson finds in these texts an "ironic shadow [that] threatens to embrace the utopian passages in its uncertain penumbra" (p. x). These meta-utopias (Morson includes More's *Utopia,* Diderot's *Supplement to Bougainville's Voyage,* and Wells's *Modern Utopia*) are fully realized "boundary works" because they are capable of eliciting multiple and even conflicting responses from readers, and because they generate the kind of uncertainty that stimulates the reader to further activity and further effort.

Morson is undoubtedly right about the determining influence of literary conventions: we "make sense" of a text by means of prevailing cultural codes, thought systems, and values that enable us to do so. As these codes and conventions change, so do our readings of texts. In our own time, for ex-

47

ample, a time in which anti-utopian attitudes and values are dominant, we tend to read many of the classical utopias as anti-utopias: Plato's *Republic* is often read today as a prototype for the modern authoritarian state; More's *Utopia* is found to be too paternalistic and warlike; Bellamy's *Looking Backward* is far too oppressively regimented and asphyxiating for readers influenced by the values of personal freedom and individual self-realization. But Morson's emphasis on the determining effect of literary and cultural codes tends to discount the concrete interaction between reader and text, a subjective encounter in which the reader's personal perspective and reading strategies also play a significant role. No text, not even an extremely closed or determinate one, has a fixed essence or settled meaning about which we can all agree; even an apparently closed text offers different perspectives from which it can be read and understood by readers who share the same cultural codes and conventions. This makes any effort at generic classification, whether we base it on formal features within the text or on reading conventions, a rather slippery undertaking. It also suggests the centrality of the reader, whose performance determines which potentials of a text are realized and which are left unrealized. As the place where the effects of a text take hold, the reader is the site of productive activity, and every interpretation of a work is also, in a very real sense, its performance.

To illustrate how literary texts elicit the participation of readers as both consumers and producers, let us look again at Wolfgang Iser's description of the reading process in *The Act of Reading*. In Iser's model of this process, a literary text is "realized" or "concretized" in a dialectical interaction between reader and text: the reader actively constructs the meaning of a text by supplying what is not explicitly stated but only implied.[15] Reading, for Iser, involves the filling in of the inevitable "gaps" or indeterminacies that arise in any text. The function of these "gaps" is to make the act of reading more productive, comparable in Iser's view to a creative act in which the reader "formulates something that is unformulated in the text and yet represents its 'intention.' "[16] Iser emphasizes that in realizing this intention the reader responds to structures already in the text, completing operations that are implicit but not completely determined by the text. Hence, Iser calls this reader an "implied reader," by which he means not an actual reader, but "a network of response-inviting structures, which impel the reader to grasp the text" (p. 34). Iser's insistence that his concept of the implied reader "has roots firmly planted in the structure of the text" (p. 34) distinguishes his model from the more radical theories of reading proposed by Barthes and Derrida, according to whom readers virtually "write" the texts they read.[17]

In Iser's model, "literary texts initiate 'performance' of meaning rather than actually formulating meaning themselves" (p. 27). As this analogy suggests, Iser conceives of reading as comparable to a theatrical performance of a dramatic text. Just as we can speak of different productions of the same play and mean that different aspects of it are brought to realization in different performances, so the reader of a literary text can realize or materialize different potentialities or possible meanings in a text. This does not mean that productions of a given text are infinite or arbitrary, or that they are all of equal value; rather, both texts and readers are constrained: texts provide a framework that "prestructures" their interpretation, and readers are historically and culturally conditioned. But what is also decisive in our interpretation of a literary text is the choices we are able to make in the process of reading—choices which grow out of our own ideological perspectives, our competence as readers, and the reading strategies we have at our disposal. These choices are limited in part by the text, but they are also open so as to allow for our active participation. As Iser puts it: "Author and reader . . . share the game of imagination, and indeed, the game will not work if the text sets out to be anything more than a set of governing rules. The reader's enjoyment begins when he himself becomes productive, that is, when the text allows him to bring his own faculties into play" (p. 108).

Iser's model of the reading process stresses the importance of a reader who is comparatively free and ideologically uncommitted. The kinds of "gaps" and indeterminacies that he values function to make the reader more productive but also to sustain reader interest and to prevent boredom. In analyzing specific works of literature, Iser favors those texts that are inconclusive, ambiguous, and open-ended. Literary utopias, by comparison, seem to be more conclusive works, works that give the reader specific instructions and are therefore more determinate in their effects. Structurally and semantically complete, utopian texts appear to be finished and closed; they are equipped with such clear meanings and messages that they seem to leave little room for reader interaction, much less for creative activity. What, if anything, then, remains implicit and unformulated in these texts that seem to strain to make everything torturously explicit for the reader?

What remains implicit and unformulated are the various effects of the social and political contradictions that utopias uncover and make transparent. Literary utopias are capable of evoking different responses in readers because, as boundary works, their functions can be seen differently, and their effects on readers can be realized in different ways. It is our own performance as readers that determines to a great extent which of their potential effects are realized. The activity of reading literary utopias, as we have seen, is essentially a dialectical process, an encounter with the unfamiliar that forces us to recognize the gaps and imperfections in the social reality that utopia tries to displace. In this process, we draw inferences, we attempt to fill in the gaps uncovered in the social fabric of society, we question the assumptions upon which the utopian solutions are based, we express our doubts about utopian claims and assurances, and, most importantly, we become aware of the irreconcilable differences between social fact and utopian vision. Literary utopias, in other words, are effectively open because they underline the importance of our own performance—our own decision-making role—as readers, inviting us, on the one hand, to give our unquestioning assent to utopian claims and forcing us, on the other hand, to assume a critical attitude toward all forms of social organization, including the utopian forms projected beyond any known time or place.

If we acknowledge the contradictory nature of utopian discourse—its conflicting methods, claims, and messages—we are more likely to pursue its inconsistencies and realize its activating impact on readers. For in seeking to formulate such all-embracing answers and such explicit solutions to social problems, utopias are bound to produce their own contradictions and inconsistencies. We may, of course, choose to disregard these contradictions and read all utopias as unambiguous representations of ideal and perfect social relations. If we choose to read utopias in this way, our evaluations will focus on their feasibility and on the desirability of realizing the utopian proposals. Such a reading strategy, however, leaves the reader in a passive posture, yields very little outside of our acceptance or rejection of the utopian suggestions, and minimizes the power of utopias to arouse and activate our critical efforts and utopian desires as readers. Readers who approach utopias in this way tend to adopt what H. G. Wells called "Aristotle's forensic method." Aristotle's petty criticisms of Plato's marriage system in the *Republic*, Wells points out, failed to take into account "that the detailed operation of this system he [Plato] put tentatively and very obscurely. His suggestions have the experimental inconsistency of an enquiring man. He left many things altogether open, and it is unfair to adopt Aristotle's forensic method and deal with his discussion as though it were a fully-worked-out project."[18] If we read literary utopias as "fully-worked-out projects," we are bound to find fault in their contradictions and inconsistencies and to reject them as imperfect. And since such rejection is usually based on values we already hold, the activity of reading utopias leaves us unchanged, our social beliefs and expectations essentially intact.

If, however, we regard literary utopias as the projections of restless and dissatisfied minds—projections that are inconclusive, playful, provocative—we are more prepared to see them as open-ended and to realize their activating potential. The activity of reading literary utopias can then become an encounter with the unfamiliar that arouses our own critical capacities and our own utopian longings. Seen this way, literary utopias are no longer diatribes that harangue the reader into embracing utopian beliefs; rather, they are dialectical interrogations of social reality that force us to recognize the provisional nature of all social values and beliefs and of our own role in formulating them. If we focus our interest on this dialectical process that both criticizes and constructs, that both defamiliarizes social reality and seeks to familiarize us with a social dream, that both intensifies existing contradictions and provides for their apparent resolution, we get a fuller sense of the contradictions at work in these texts. We recognize that, in situating the reader on the very boundary between an unacceptable social reality and an impossible utopian dream, utopian fiction *seeks* to have an activating effect—a continual engagement of the reader with social reality—that requires the reader to go beyond what is represented in the text and perhaps even to modify her own social beliefs. Utopias may be read as a call to action by some readers, but they depend for their effect on the reader's readiness to question routine habits of perception, to entertain other values and other expectations, and to change. To specify the contradictory processes at the heart of utopian narrative and to clarify their potential effects on readers, we must examine in the next chapter the kind of dialectical reading that these texts require and reward.

3

The Role of the Reader
Between Possibility and Necessity

For the first time in my life, I was having my fill of the pleasure of the eyes without any of that sense of incongruity, that dread of approaching ruin, which had always beset me hitherto when I had been amongst the beautiful works of art of the past. . . . . Here I could enjoy everything without an after-thought of the injustice and miserable toil which made my leisure; the ignorance and dulness of life which went to make my keen appreciation of history; the tyranny and the struggle full of fear and mishap which went to make my romance.

— WILLIAM MORRIS, *News from Nowhere*

The increased concern in recent literary theory with the activity of "reading" entails an important shift from studying what a text *is* to studying what it *does:* a shift from a view of reading as an object-oriented activity to an understanding of it as a subjective process, a reciprocal transaction between reader and text in which one affects the other. At one time stigmatized as "the affective fallacy,"[1] this orientation has since become the foundation of various reader-oriented approaches. These insist, generally, that the meaning of any text—verbal, visual, or aural—cannot be fully grasped by an analysis of its formal patterns, nor by an explication of its contents, but must also be understood

54

to involve its effects: how a text engages us and positions us in attending to its messages, how it may activate and liberate us in this process, or how it may leave us passive and complacent. In taking up these questions, I will try to show that literary utopias are best understood in terms of a dialectical model of the reader/text relationship, one in which reader and text are welded together in mutual dependence: the act of reading is guided by textual structures, but these structures cannot be actualized in the absence of a reader's performance. Reading, in other words, cannot be reduced to either the components of the text or the responses of readers, but is a process of mutual implication and mutual determination. In reading literary utopias we are guided by the text and by our own reading strategies, but the purpose of this guidance, I contend, is to set us free, not only from textual constraints, but from forms of manipulation and control in the world outside the text. The application of a dialectical model of reading allows us to counter the prevailing view that literary utopias are entirely dogmatic and programmatic in their effects on readers and to provide a typology of the implied reader that these texts require—a more active reader who is both the target of the contradictions that utopias take up and the site of their eventual resolution.

Because literary utopias are dialogical in structure and inspiration, they also call for an acutely dialectical perception on the part of the reader. As expositions of social problems and tensions, utopias function to defamiliarize or "make strange" existing social contradictions for cognitive purposes. The essential effect of this defamiliarization is to make the reader aware that she is not merely a passive observer in a reified world, but an agent acting in an open world that has been formed, and can be transformed, by human beings. Thus, in terms of their effects, literary utopias are "open" not merely in the sense that they allow for different interpretations, but, more importantly, in the sense that they situate the reader in a critically distanced and hence liberated relationship to what they represent. This kind of "openness" aims at producing a heightened sense of awareness in the reader, an awareness that allows her to see all forms of organization—social, political, aesthetic—as contingent and provisional. The effect of this critical distancing is to remind us that whatever "is"—whether it be the social arrangements exposed in the text or our own present moment in history—is historical, provisional, and therefore changeable.

At the same time, however, literary utopias also provide us with unambiguous alternatives and "closed" solutions. While they critically distance prevailing social values, they also formulate new values; while they negate existing norms, they also prescribe new norms to replace the old ones. Their critical function of heightening our awareness of social contradictions is apparently offset by an escapist function that lessens our social concern, seeming to resolve social discrepancies by means of a timeless, all-embracing solution. Thus, the twofold strategy of literary utopias entails both the unmasking of prevailing forms of social manipulation, domination, and containment (the critical edge of defamiliarization) *and* the projection of a utopian dream in which all forms of alienation and manipulation are dramatically reversed or negated.

Failure to take into account the activating potential of this twofold strategy on readers has resulted in a tendency toward one-sided readings of utopian literature. These readings can be countered, it seems to me, if we suspend our deeply ingrained habit of reading literary texts as static or fixed objects for analysis and read them instead in terms of the effects produced by their textual strategies and ideological structuring. The *activity* of reading a text, as this term suggests, can never be merely a matter of passively decoding it but must also consider the ideological effects produced in the subjective interplay between reader and text. In the case of literary utopias, these effects are produced by the twofold strategy described above and by the contradictions this strategy generates. All utopias proceed by drawing attention to the inconsistencies between utopian and pre-utopian forms of social organization. But in doing this, they involve the reader in a number of important contradictions: they are informed both with a critical desire for social change and rejuvenation and with an escapist desire for permanent and perfect solutions; they envision an alternative that is presented as "real" and practical but that is also "nowhere" in space and time; they set out to reconcile all social contradictions and to eliminate antagonisms and end up demonstrating their inescapability. Contrasts, discrepancies, incongruities, and contradictions—these are the raw materials from which all utopias are constructed and the essential conditions in society that inspire them. Without them utopias would be impossible. For if the desired utopian harmony were ever realized, the disparities and contradictions that fuel all utopian activity would cease to exist, and, presumably, utopias themselves would disappear. The paradox, as has often been observed, is that utopian literature would itself have no place and no function within a fully realized utopian society since the oppositions and contrasts on which it depends would by definition no longer exist.

To derive the activating effects of these contradictions, we must look beyond the apparently "closed" form of literary utopias; we must go beyond their reductive solutions and try to disclose meanings that are not objective properties of the text, but which are nevertheless an important part of their critical impact on readers. Such disclosure will allow us to identify what it is about utopian works that enables them to say more than they apparently say, to have an effect that transcends their formulaic solutions and dogmatic assertions. Such a procedure is justified since any text, no matter how manipulative and one-dimensional it may seem, cannot say all that it means: its meanings are also enabled by what it doesn't say, by what it attempts to exclude or to conceal.

Thus, even a programmatic text cannot entirely control its reception: such a text can give rise to interpretations not foreseen by the author. The first step in uncovering the activating potential of literary utopias, then, is to shift our perspective away from a view of the text as a determinate object and to focus instead on the less determinate interrelationship between reader and text.

Such a shift in perspective is the central tenet of "reception aesthetics," or reader-oriented criticism. The leading proponents of this approach, or more accurately, these approaches—Eco, Iser, Holland, Fish, Culler, Bleich, and others—have developed various models of the reader/text relationship.[2] Despite the important differences that distinguish these approaches from one another, they can be seen to share basic presuppositions that set them apart from more traditional kinds of criticism. Essentially, these theorists question the existence of an objective or fixed meaning in a text. Instead, they argue, the meaning of any work of art is not so much given in the text as it is "concretized" or "realized" or even "created" by the reader. There is, in other words, no determinate meaning that reveals itself in the same way to each individual reader: any text has a number of potential meanings. Thus, for these theorists, any text—verbal, visual, aural—is a series of cues, a sequence of organized images, signs, and sounds that the reader materializes in the act of reading. Without the reader's active and continuous participation, there would, in fact, be no "text" at all.[3]

But while these reader-oriented theorists generally agree on the important role played by the reader in the interpretative process, they also disagree in fundamental ways about the level of control exercised by the text in this process. The tremendous debate and disunity over the question of whether textual structures or readers' performances have priority has led to a situation in which the relationship between reader and text is often blurred. Eco and Iser, for example, whose approaches to reading are most influential in this study, see this relationship as a dialectical partnership between reader and text in which neither textual structure nor reader's performance has priority. For these theorists, reader and text are bonded together in mutual dependence: the structural components of the text control the reader, and the activity of the reader completes textual structures. Since neither can be realized in the absence of the other and since each is the obverse of the other, the act of reading cannot be reduced to causal paradigms in which either text or reader has clear priority. Such a dialectical formulation of the reader/text relationship recognizes both the constraints of and the indeterminacies in the text, thus enhancing the role of the reader. In Iser's model, a text encodes an "implied reader," who, as we have seen, is anticipated by the text and whose responses are "prestructured" to some extent; Eco acknowledges similar constraints in the "discursive structures" and "textual strategies" of a text, whose "Model Reader" is to a significant extent a product of textual processing.[4] The virtue of this approach is that it recognizes the reality of textual structures (in effect, of the text) at the same time that it recognizes the reader's role. For other proponents of reader-response criticism, a text is regarded as far less constraining, and its meaning, therefore, becomes increasingly a product of the reader's interpretation. For Fish and Bleich, for example, reading is not so much a matter of uncovering potential meaning in a text as it is a matter of experiencing effects; and these effects are a function more of the reader, or "communities of readers," than of anything we can locate in the texts themselves.[5]

In view of this fundamental disagreement about the determinacy or indeterminacy of literary texts, it is helpful to begin by acknowledging that some texts exert more and some less control in the interpretative process. It is also helpful to distinguish, as Eco does in *The Role of the Reader*, between "open" texts that invite the participation of the reader as "a purposeful strategy of openness" and "closed" texts that seek to elicit a more precise response (p. 40). Simply stated, different kinds of texts require and reward different kinds of performances from readers. "Open" texts require a more active and a more cooperative reader. Such texts force the reader to make a maximum number of interpretative choices. Since such texts often set out to subvert established codes and conventions, they require a productive reader, one who is willing to make inferences, to assume the task of resolving ambiguities, and to draw his own conclusions.

Such "open" texts may be further distinguished by the purpose or end for which openness is employed. In much of modernist literature, for example, openness functions primarily to foreground formal possibilities; temporal dislocations and narrative disruptions in these texts are designed to disturb reader passivity in order to liberate the reader from the bonds of illusionism and to reveal the artificiality of all forms. This same strategy, however, can also be used for different ends: to disturb reader passivity and alter reader perceptions, not primarily about the nature and working of art, but about the social and political world in which the reader lives. Producing this kind of ideological effect is a crucial function of the twofold strategy of literary utopias: to sharpen our perception of sociopolitical contradictions and to suggest possible solutions. The critical impact of this strategy is to make the reader more conscious of his own role in society and in history.

But the "open" text, whether reflexive or reflective of social and political concerns, is not open to just any reading. On the contrary, for Eco there is a "Model Reader" who can be extrapolated from such a text; for in trying to deny a passive reader/text relationship, the "open" text gains a measure of control over its interpretation. As Eco puts it: "An open text, however 'open' it be, cannot afford whatever interpretation"; rather, "an open text outlines a 'closed' project of its Model

Reader as a component of its structural strategy" (p. 9). Thus, paradoxically, the "open" text exercises a greater degree of determinacy over the reader's interpretation. "If there is a 'jouissance du texte,'" Eco observes with reference to Barthes's essay, "it cannot be aroused and implemented except by a text producing all the paths of its 'good' reading (no matter how many, no matter how much determined in advance)" (p. 10).

"Closed" texts, on the other hand, "obsessively aim at arousing a precise response on the part of more or less precise empirical readers," according to Eco (p. 8). Such texts tend to make fewer demands on the reader: the story develops univocally, the reader follows a precise and predictable path, the passage of meaning from text to reader is untroubled. Since these texts tend to stay within the rules, conventions, and contexts that govern them, they do not question our "normal" habits of perception and do not transgress our expectations. Instead, they seek to conceal their fictive status and leave the reader undisturbed in his basic assumptions about art and society. The ideological effect of such a text is to confirm existing values and norms, to satisfy reader expectations, and to allow the reader to remain a passive and satisfied consumer. For Eco, however, it is because "these texts are potentially speaking to everyone" that they are "in fact open to any possible 'aberrant' decoding," by which he means an interpretation not envisaged by the author (p. 8). Thus, surprisingly enough, "closed" texts "can give rise to the most unforeseeable interpretations, at least at the ideological level," according to Eco (p. 8). Such texts are "immoderately 'open'" for Eco, because different readers, with different priorities, tastes, and ideological perspectives, will single out different structures and perceive them in different contexts. Eco analyzes the Superman myth and James Bond novels as examples of "closed" texts that yield divergent ideological readings without betraying their structural integrity.

61

In applying Eco's distinction between "open" and "closed" texts to literary utopias, we find that some models—for example, More's *Utopia*, Wells's *Modern Utopia*, and the ambiguous utopias of Le Guin and Piercy—tend to be more or less "open," while others—such as Cabet's *Voyage to Icaria*, Bellamy's *Looking Backward*, and Skinner's *Walden Two*—tend to be more or less "closed." This distinction is somewhat misleading, however, since all utopias contain features of both the "open" and the "closed" text. Formally, all utopias (even open ones) are structured like Eco's closed texts: they expose social problems and formulate solutions, inviting the reader to embrace utopian values. In this sense, all utopias are closed and complete. At the same time, however, all utopias (including the closed ones) produce the disturbing effects of Eco's open texts: they invalidate our assumptions about the nature of social relations, they seek to alter our perceptions of social life, they force us to rethink our relationship to history and to the sociopolitical system in which we live. Thus, even though literary utopias are constructed like closed texts that try to elicit a precise response, they also force us to assume a more critical and detached position toward all social propositions, including the ones they offer. In reading literary utopias, then, we are certainly constrained: we are asked to suspend our critical faculties and convert to utopian values; but we are also asked to become more critical and more disbelieving since the utopian solutions are themselves paradoxical, or, at least, are not without their own contradictions. Indeed, it is just where utopias seem most closed—in their formulas for the perfect society—that they are in fact most open (as present-day responses to many classical utopias demonstrate). Conversely, it is just where utopian texts are apparently most open—in their dialectical structuring—that we discover the text exercising a considerable degree of determinacy over how it will be read (as Eco puts it, "producing all the paths of its 'good' reading"). Yet the net effect of this determinacy is to place the reader in a quandary which he can resolve only by taking up the issues at the heart of the text.

We may say, then, that literary utopias suspend us between two options. They seek to elicit our consent to utopian values, and we may choose to give that consent and follow the path of conversion outlined for us in the text. Since utopias also provide insights that undermine our easy conversion, however, we may find the utopian solutions ultimately insufficient to resolve the social problems they encounter. It is the activating potential of these conflicting options that can make the experience of reading literary utopias thought-provoking and unsettling. For in suspending us between these two options, utopias also enfold us in an open-ended dialectical inquiry concerning social possibility and social necessity, an inquiry that illuminates and intensifies social tensions and disparities at the same time that it appears to resolve them.

To illustrate how even closed utopias engage the reader in this kind of open-ended dialectical inquiry, let us briefly consider Bellamy's *Looking Backward: 2000–1887* (1887).[6] In this work Bellamy envisions a utopian future that looks back on the glaring contradictions of nineteenth-century industrial life in Boston. Julian West, Bellamy's insomniac dreamer, "wakes up" both physically and morally in the twentieth century and is astonished to find a "glorious new Boston" situated on the site of the grimy old one. The changes he observes everywhere are truly startling: "In the time of one generation," he exclaims, "men laid aside the social traditions of barbarians, and assumed a social order worthy of rational and human beings" (p. 233). West discovers further that capitalism has been recognized as pure folly and abruptly abandoned; the entire country has been reorganized into a vast, efficient "industrial army," dominated by a technocratic bureaucracy and indoctrinated by propagandistic sermons delivered on the "telephone." In general, Bellamy's vision is of a highly centralized and "closed" society that resembles, in many ways, the anti-utopian parodies it generated. As a blue-print for social perfection, Bellamy's vision is extremely con-straining and debilitating; few readers could consider it ideal or even desirable. As an extremely "closed" text, *Looking Backward* aims at a precise goal: to demonstrate the absolute superiority of utopian institutions and to convert the reader to this point of view. But this is precisely what readers are unable to do, given the authoritarian nature of Bellamy's vi-sion and the total regimentation of life that it entails. Unable to convert to the utopian values explicitly outlined in the text, the reader is also unable to read the text as a blueprint for social action. Thus, she is forced to assume a more detached position from which Bellamy's vision can be evaluated as a kind of intellectual experiment in which two opposing and incongruous images of social life are juxtaposed in order to produce certain cognitive effects. Seen this way, Bellamy's closed text becomes another kind of text, an open text that is designed to interrogate the nature of social life and social change. If we now read the text as a dialectical and therefore inconclusive exploration of social possibilities, then the very shortcomings of Bellamy's vision can become the occasion for the reader to assume a more critical and a more active posi-tion in relation to the text.

This more active role for the reader is indicated by the kinds of cognitive effects that West's venture into utopia produces in him. Among the many changes that West encounters in his new world is a change in the very experience of reading. To familiarize himself with his strange new surroundings, West reads a work of fiction ostensibly written by a twentieth-cen-tury utopian writer, Berrian. What West finds shocking about this work is "not so much what was in the book but what was left out of it." West realizes that what is absent from Berrian's book is "all the effects drawn from the contrasts of wealth and poverty, education and ignorance, coarseness and refine-ment, high and low." (p. 137). West assures us that Berrian's work has great literary merit, but he tells us very little else about it and we are left to imagine what a work "without the effects drawn from contrasts" would be like. What is certain, however, is that Berrian's work is unlike *Looking Backward,* since it lacks precisely the oppositions, contrasts, and disparities that are so essential to Bellamy's text. When West tries to describe the effects of Berrian's purified fiction, he cannot do so without invoking Dickens, a favorite author of these future Bostonians in spite of the many contrasts and conflicts in his works. It is only by juxtaposing these two authors, representing utopian and pre-utopian forms of social life, and by observing their differences, that West is able to see with a new sharpness: "With a clearness which I had not been able before to attain, I saw now the past and present, like contrasting pictures, side by side" (p. 118). The crucial effect produced by these "contrasting pictures" is both unsettling and illuminating for West and is, of course, precisely the effect that Bellamy's text seeks to have on its readers. West describes it as "an effect no others could have had, to intensify, by force of contrasts, my appreciation of the strangeness of my present environment" (p. 118). West's experience as a reader within the text—reading Berrian and Dickens "side by side"—parallels our own situation and experience as readers of *Looking Backward:* we, too, are readers who have been abruptly displaced into a strange land, a land purified of all contrasts and contradictions, the startling effect of which is to intensify our sense of the oppositions and contradictions that mar and constrain social life.

The kind of intensified perception that this dialectical process is intended to produce is made evident toward the end of *Looking Backward* when West wakes up one morning and finds himself back in the dystopian Boston of 1887. As he walks through the streets he realizes for the first time the absurdities and inconsistencies that had previously appeared natural and routine. "I had to stop and pull myself together," he exclaims, "such power had been in that vision of the future to make the real Boston strange" (p. 255). West's experience in utopia has radically altered his perceptions. Prior to his awakening in utopia, he had been a "proper" Bostonian, a member of the privileged class—complacent, superficial, self-absorbed. Now, upon his return, it is as if "the scales had fallen from [his] eyes" (p. 265). Glaring discrepancies and inequities are now painfully apparent to him: stores that compete in selling useless and unwanted items, industries whose practices are wasteful and immoral, banks—the "life-blood" of pre-utopian Boston—that now appear ridiculous and absurd. Everywhere he looks West sees "the spectre of Uncertainty," and the only protection society offers against this uncertainty is "some new scheme of life insurance" (p. 263). In this dream, West has truly "awakened" to the real world around him, a liberating experience made possible by his venture into utopian alternatives.

West's experience in utopia shows how utopian literature controls its readers, but it also shows how this control liberates the reader—how utopias arouse a response that is guided by a dialectical logic that sees everything in terms of oppositions and contradictions. West's recognition of the discrepancies that constrain social relations is made possible by utopia's power to heighten our social awareness and to alter our social perceptions. When he awakens again, this time back in the twentieth century, West realizes that his "return to the nineteenth century had been a dream, and [his] presence in the twentieth was a reality" (p. 271). For West, the "evil reality" of history turns into dream, and the "fair dream" of utopia turns into reality; for West, at least, this inversion of dream and reality makes it easy and convenient to convert to utopia, to escape the nightmare world of nineteenth-century Boston. But for us, the readers outside the text, this inversion of dream and reality has a different function and produces a different effect. Unlike West, we do not have the opportunity to leave history behind and move into a fully established utopia. Instead, we must return to the teeming world of contrasts and contradictions, the world of Dickens rather than the world of Berrian. Yet it is here, in this contradictory world of history, activity, and potentiality, that the static utopian dream has its most important effect: for in blurring the distinction between history and utopian dream, Bellamy suggests that history is a dream and utopia is real. The productive effect of this confusion is to startle the reader, to suspend her momentarily between an impossible dream, suddenly made real, and an intolerable social reality, suddenly made into a dream. In this way, existing social forms are made to appear arbitrary and therefore changeable. And it is by thus inverting social reality and utopian dream that all utopias make us more sensitive to our own moment in history *as* a moment in history—that is, as a human project that is provisional and open-ended—thereby increasing our awareness of the historicity of all forms of social organization.

The important changes that West undergoes as a result of his utopian dream exemplify the way in which utopian literature attempts to intensify our perception of social contradictions in order to change our social views. These changes are controlled by the essential utopian activity of comparing and contrasting two incongruous and incompatible images of social life. These contrasts constitute the essential "conditions in the text" that shape or "prestructure" the experience of reading utopias. To ensure that the process of comparison takes place, literary utopias employ another textual strategy—the presence of two conflicting perspectives, or two voices, that reflect opposing views on utopian values. One perspective is that of a representative from inside utopia, who, like Dr. Leete in *Looking Backward*, functions as a guide who takes us on a tour of utopian institutions and achievements; the other perspective is that of a visitor or traveler to utopia, who, like Julian West, is a representative of the world outside utopia, an enervating world whose scars the visitor usually bears. The role of the visitor is primarily to listen, to ask questions from time to time, to express disbelief or astonishment, and, in the end, to embrace (or reject) utopian values. The relationship between these two voices may be contentious and argumentative, or it may be rather one-sided, in which case the guide dominates the dialogue and the visitor asks mainly perfunctory questions that keep the dialogue moving. In More's *Utopia*, for example, the relationship between the guide, Hythloday, and the listener, "More," is contentious. "More" listens to Hythloday's exposition of life among the Utopians and is intrigued by Utopian values, but he remains skeptical about many of Hythloday's claims and assertions. A similar skeptical attitude is evident in the relationship between the narrator and his traveling companion in Wells's *Modern Utopia*. Even in Skinner's *Walden Two*, an extremely closed utopia, the visitor (Burris) expresses some serious doubts about Frazier, the founder and guiding spirit of this relentlessly conditioned utopian community. Burris does convert in the end, but he does so with considerable apprehension. In view of Frazier's personality problems and the power inherent in his "science of human engineering," Burris's fears are well-founded. Even in a closed utopia, then, the contentious relationship between guide and visitor can generate some ambivalence about utopian solutions in the reader's mind, cautioning against easy conversion to utopian values.

It is because this relationship between guide and visitor in the text parallels our own situation relative to the text that the experience of reading literary utopias is often equated with the visitor's journey to utopia. Morson, for example, argues that "most utopias are constructed as allegories for the process of reading them."[7] He finds that "utopias characteristically set up a metaphorical equation of the journey to the utopian world with the reading of the utopian work" (p. 96). This identification of the reader and visitor is based on the fact that the reader, like the visitor, journeys through space or time in order to experience firsthand the fantastic innovations and transformations that characterize utopian life. The reader's task, like that of the visitor, is simply to listen to the guide's exposition and to embrace or deny utopia by accepting or rejecting its claims. Morson sees this as an effective means by which the utopian text seeks to control and manipulate its readers. For if the reader chooses to reject the utopian way of life, Morson points out, she does so at considerable cost: by rejecting utopia, the reader forfeits equality, freedom, and justice and opts for the corruption, exploitation, and injustice that the utopian text offers as the only alternative.

This typology of the reader suggests itself in view of the unambiguously superior values that utopia represents. But it seems appropriate only for the most closed utopian texts, texts which seem to reduce the role of the reader to that of passive consumer. It obviously does not apply to the more ambiguous utopias that Morson classifies as "meta-utopias," those texts in which the contrasting viewpoints of guide and listener remain contested and unresolved. In these meta-utopias the reader's role cannot be equated with either perspective in the text, since each is deficient when viewed from the other perspective; rather, the reader's role in these texts is to examine more critically the claims and counterclaims that these perspectives present. In interrogating these claims on his own, the reader assumes a position that is outside, or more precisely in between, the opposing perspectives and the contrasting worlds they represent.

But this is so, to a certain extent, even in the programmatic and more dogmatic utopias that formulate unambiguous answers for their readers. Clearly, Morson's typology of the reader assumes that most utopias are more or less self-cancelling efforts: they uncover social problems and prescribe explicit and final answers. But once we see the relationship between social problems and utopian solutions in terms of a mutual illumination and intensification, as I have tried to suggest we must, then each naturally becomes subject to a critical evaluation from the point of view of the other. The reader's interest can readily shift from the utopian formulations themselves to the dialectical interplay between social criticism and utopian dream—a shift that allows the reader to respond to the twofold strategy behind all utopian undertaking. This shift allows us to recognize the deficiencies that are revealed in the visitor's world and at the same time to look for the deficiencies or inadequacies that the utopian solution seeks to conceal. The reader's role, in other words, cannot and should not be limited either to the perspective of the traveler to utopia or to that of the guide, but should be recognized as implicit in the interplay between these contrasting viewpoints and the contrasting social values they represent. Seen this way, the full effect of a utopian text cannot be limited to either acceptance or rejection of explicit utopian answers, but consists rather in the implied utopian activity that sets a familiar world against an unfamiliar one in order to explore the parameters of social possibility.

Louis Marin has identified the two conflicting semantic operations of utopian texts that underlie the more overt textual strategies I have been describing. "The critical power of utopia," he writes, "derives, on the one hand, from the (metaphorical) projection of existing reality into an 'elsewhere' that cannot be situated in historical time or in geographical space; and, on the other, from (metonymic) displacement, that is to say, from an accentual variation within the reality it expresses."[8] The twin operations of "metaphorical projection" and "metonymic displacement" constitute, for Marin, fundamental ways in which utopian discourse establishes the conflicting relationship between critical social analysis and utopian fiction.

Marin's distinction between metaphorical and metonymic

operations in utopian narrative is best understood in the context of Roman Jakobson's view that metaphor and metonymy constitute binary oppositions. In his well-known essay "Two Aspects of Language and Two Types of Aphasic Disturbances," Jakobson claimed that linguistic activity develops primarily either through a process of selection, of choosing among similarities (a paradigmatic process), or through contiguity, a process of combining the elements chosen (a syntagmatic process). "The development of discourse," Jakobson writes, "may take place along two different semantic lines: one topic may lead to another through their similarity or through contiguity. The metaphorical way would be the more appropriate for the first case and the metonymic for the second, since they find their most condensed expression in metaphor and metonymy respectively."[9] For Jakobson, these two modes of discourse are in conflict and competition with one another so that one usually dominates a given form of discourse. He finds, for example, that metaphor is the dominant mode in poetry, romanticism, symbolism, and surrealism, while metonymy is dominant in those forms in which verisimilitude takes precedence, for example, in film or in works of realism and cubism.

But these modes of discourse need not necessarily be as exclusive as Jakobson suggests. Literary utopias, for example, combine both. As "boundary works," they provide us with a combination of heterogeneous materials—essay, moral philosophy, imaginative fiction, political and theoretical tracts—and make use of both metaphorical and metonymic modes of discourse. In constructing a fictive nowhere—a blessed isle or happy future—utopias project an "other" place that is similar to the world of its composition but also different in many respects. In projecting this "other" place, the utopian author is not bound by the strictures of realism and is able to invent an imaginary time or place that is intended to transcend the limits of historical time or place. But, as we have already seen,

71

literary utopias also necessarily evoke a more familiar time and place, contiguous with the author's environment. This historical background is evoked by numerous references to figures, places, and events that occur in the author's society. As "metonymic displacements," literary utopias reproduce a referential background, or a kind of historical mirror, against which the utopian projection stands out and achieves its significance. Without this metonymic pole, the remarkable transformations in utopia would not be apparent to the reader. The utopian innovations delineated in Book II of More's *Utopia,* for example, need to be compared to the social miseries sketched out in Book I in order to have their critical impact on readers. Similarly, Morris's *News from Nowhere* and Bellamy's *Looking Backward* project fictive futures which must be read against the metonymic backgrounds of nineteenth-century industrial life. Berrian's utopian novel, as we have seen, achieves significance for West only when he compares it to the novels of Dickens and to the social world they represent. To achieve their critical effects on readers, then, literary utopias engage the reader in a dialectical interplay between conflicting modes of discourse that both reproduce a "real" or historical background and envision a marvelous departure from it, a deviation that defamiliarizes it, makes it seem strange.

In a very real sense, then, utopian narrative represents a conjunction of metonymic and metaphorical operations the effect of which is to suspend the reader between the actual and the imaginary, between the concrete and the abstract, between realism and fantasy. It is this suspension between the familiar and the unfamiliar—between contiguity and rupture, confirmation and dislocation—that produces the disturbing and unsettling effects that literary utopias can have on readers. Suvin's conception of literary utopias as "positive negations" recognizes the same opposition between social criticism and utopian vision as the heart of the matter. Robert

Elliott has described this conflict in terms of a dialectic between satire and hope. "Satire and utopia," he writes, "are not really separable, the one a critique of the real world in the name of something better, the other a hopeful construct of a better world that might be. The hope feeds the criticism, the criticism the hope."[10]

In terms of Eco's distinction between "open" and "closed" texts, literary utopias can now be recognized to effectively combine the strategies of both in order to startle and confound the reader. In order to make the reader more aware of social contradictions and disparities, utopias employ narrative strategies that are themselves contradictory and inconsistent. Utopia is synonymous with a desire for social change but constructs a system that denies any further changes; it sets out to liberate us from forms of social manipulation and containment but provides us with a system that, in its constraints and manipulations, also becomes oppressive, is itself constraining and manipulative; it unmasks existing ideology as contradictory but then masks the significance of this recognition with an ideology that pretends to be the end of ideology. In presenting itself to us as a fully realized project, utopia attempts to disguise its fictive status and to deny its own contingent role in the historical process. Thus, utopias plant the seeds of their own criticism, and the result is that the reader is able to challenge utopia on the basis of its ahistorical locality.

The utopian effort to deny the possibility of problems and difficulties within its borders should in itself caution us against accepting utopian propositions and formulations at face value. For in formulating social alternatives, literary utopias not only unmask existing ideology, they also prescribe new ideologies, new systems of values and attitudes that are intended to replace the old ones. The new ideology, however, is not subjected to the same critical analysis as the old. Rather, it is established beyond any known time or place, en-

73

closed by firm boundaries as a static and unassailable solution. And this privileged, ahistorical status that utopia reserves for itself is not free from its own contradictions and its own ideological interests.

In his well-known definition of "the utopian mentality" as "a state of mind that is incongruous with the state of reality in which it occurs," Karl Mannheim indicates the opposing functions and effects of ideology and utopia.[11] In Mannheim's view, ideology is a nonrevolutionary form of "false consciousness": unaware of the potential for social change, it tries to perpetuate the status quo as the best of all possible worlds and thus alienates us from our own possibilities. Utopia, by contrast, is revolutionary: it seeks constantly to transcend the bonds and boundaries of ideology and endeavors to liberate us from blind habit and routine. For Mannheim, utopia is always based on the recognition that we are more than what existing ideology allows us to be, and it exhorts us to change existing social arrangements. In this way, utopia has the power to reveal existing social forms and social arrangements as historical and therefore changeable.

But this useful distinction between ideology and utopia should not lead us to accept utopia at face value and to fail to recognize its own inescapable ideological contamination. For while it is true that utopia functions to reveal the historicity of social life, it also projects a new order, a new system of social relations which is presented as the best of all possible worlds— in fact, a new ideology. In thus failing to attain consciousness of its own role in the historical process, utopia becomes like the ideology it attempts to expose and invalidate. In short, utopia tries to conceal its own recognitions about the historicity of social life by denying the reality of history within its own borders.

This apparent contradiction should be construed, however, not as a shortcoming of utopian discourse but rather as part of the conflicting and contradictory strategy by which utopian texts seek to arouse a more active response from their readers. Rather than constituting a sanguine vision of social perfection that eliminates all contradictions and resolves all oppositions, utopia can now be seen as an intensification of them; rather than constituting a series of formulaic solutions that merely require our consent, utopia can now be grasped as an inconsistent and inconclusive interplay between social history and utopian possibility that forces us to assume a more critical position.

The activity of reading literary utopias, then, ultimately involves us in a dialectical interplay between history and utopia, the object of which is to put us in touch with social contradictions. The method of this exercise is to subject existing social forms to fictive permutations. If we participate actively in this exercise, we will not be content with the formulaic utopian values of order, efficiency, and certainty, but will subject these values to further interrogation. In this way we will be able to uncover the problems and deficiencies that these cloudless visions of perfection attempt to conceal: their reductiveness, their exclusiveness, their contradictory status, their arrogant claim to reconcile the differences between the real and the ideal. Once we recognize the deficiencies within the boundaries of utopia itself, then reading utopias can no longer be simply a question of accepting or rejecting utopian values: in rejecting utopia we are left with the intolerable social reality that it has exposed, and conversion to utopia implies that we can get outside of time and history—a possibility that, even in utopia, exists nowhere. Unable simply to convert to utopia, the reader is also unable to return unchanged to the actual world of strife, conflict, and history. Thus, suspended in the gap between history and utopia, or between "now" and "nowhere," the reader is provoked to engage on her own terms the problems, the aspirations, and the potential solutions that constitute the inspiration of utopian thinking and of utopian activity.

If we choose to read literary utopias as straightforward representations of perfect social relations, we will fail to realize their efficacy as works built on contradiction. Like many readers, we will find most literary utopias to be facile, constraining, and life-denying. Most readers, for example, find Bellamy's vision of life in a vast, efficient "industrial army" to be not a blueprint for human happiness or a vision of imaginative social possibilities but a terrible nightmare that reduces rather than enhances human possibilities. As a description of social perfection, Bellamy's vision is indeed faulty. But if we read the shortcomings in Bellamy's utopia in terms of how they reveal and illuminate social contradictions, indeed, in terms of our own inability to dream our way cleanly out of our historical situation, then it becomes another kind of text, one that has the power to reveal the full complexity of the problem even while it tries to conceal it. If we read Bellamy's text this way, then we must assume a more active role and try to "complete" the vision of utopia that in Bellamy's version remains incomplete.

What remains incomplete in Bellamy's vision has been spelled out in great detail in William Morris's dialectical reading of Bellamy's text. In *News from Nowhere*, Morris attempts to fill in what Bellamy's text excludes, to reveal what Bellamy's text conceals. Instead of Bellamy's progress-oriented future society, Morris proposes "an epoch of rest." He counters Bellamy's faith in the benefits of technology by showing that technology can also pollute life and create misery. He challenges Bellamy's ideal of a centralized society by projecting a decentralized social ideal that is based on sensual pleasure and participatory democracy. Unlike Bellamy, who left the matter of personal relations rather abstract, Morris provides a vivid and detailed picture of them. And where Bellamy failed to account for the crucial question of the transition from pre-utopian to utopian social relations, Morris attempts to fill in this gap with a long chapter entitled "How the

Change Came." Morris's critical response to Bellamy, in other words, attempted to complete Bellamy's fragmented and inconclusive vision; Morris tried to reveal the exclusions that a dialectical reading of Bellamy's text uncovers and intensifies. A similar response on the part of the reader can also unfold the full significance and complexity of the issues raised by literary utopias and can make the experience of reading utopias, even extremely closed and constraining ones, more active and rewarding.

This means, of course, that Morris's utopian vision should also be subjected to this kind of dialectical reading, an interrogation that uncovers contradictions and envisions alternatives. For in eliminating all structure, technology, and organization, Morris's dream is not without its own problems. There is, for example, no economic base for Morris's idealized version of fourteenth-century social life, and the effort to locate utopia in the historical past is bound to produce other contradictions. In short, each utopian vision, whether it is formulated as an "open" or as a "closed" text, discloses certain social possibilities at the same time that it represses others; each unmasks certain social limitations at the same time that it masks others. In reading literary utopias, we should not be content either to embrace or to reject utopian formulations and propositions, but should endeavor to uncover their limitations and identify their exclusions and in the process construct our own utopian visions—if not on paper, then at least in our own imaginations. By responding more actively to the inevitable gaps in the social and political fabric of all utopian production, we participate more fully in the open-ended and inconclusive interplay between our historical limitations and our utopian dreams, which is ultimately the real interest in the activity of reading and producing utopian alternatives.

4

More's *Utopia*
The Logic of Contradictions

*Significant utopian writings are in permanent dialogue
with the readers, they are open-ended—as in More.*

— D A R K O S U V I N , *Metamorphoses of Science Fiction*

The ambivalent impact of
More's *Utopia* is evident in the host of conflicting interpretations and in the controversies that this apparently simple
book has generated over the years. At various times More's
Best State of a Commonwealth and the New Island of Utopia, as it is
subtitled, has been read as a revolutionary book that proposes radical changes, as a reactionary book that longs
nostalgically for a simple monastic life and medieval ideals,
and as a playful and ironic book that endorses no particular
world view. The tangle of conflicting interpretations includes
Catholic readings, Protestant readings, Socialist readings,
Communist readings, and a host of other interpretative readings. Even individual readers have offered different interpretations at different times. J. H. Hexter, one of the edi-
tors of the Yale edition of More's work, has concluded on
separate occasions that *Utopia* is a politically progressive and
historically conscious work, a liberal book that makes modest
proposals, and an escapist book that makes no serious proposals.[1] Hexter has since sought to "impose some salutary
restrictions on the free flight of fancy of interpreting scholars"

by insisting that the meaning of *Utopia* can be determined conclusively once we subject More's text to "exhaustive contextual analysis."[2] Hexter's aim is to delimit the possible readings of More's text by locating its meaning in authorial intention; but in this effort he minimizes the enigmas, puzzles, and ironies that characterize *Utopia* and that have made the experience of reading More's text equivocal, resonant, and semantically rich for many readers.

In view of the diverse and conflicting readings that *Utopia* has generated, it seems more appropriate that we begin by suspending our search for a correct and conclusive interpretation and focus instead on the conditions in More's text that allow for this spectrum of possible readings. For in spite of its seeming simplicity, reductiveness, and programmatic tone, *Utopia* remains an elusive text, and part of its identity lies precisely in its elusiveness. Indeed, the paradoxes and contradictions within More's text are effective precisely because they stimulate and spur the reader's "free flight of fancy." In restricting the potential meanings of *Utopia*, we reduce its significance. No single reading of *Utopia* (or of any literary work) can exhaust its potential meaning, since each reading imposes its own interests and priorities and relates the text to its own framework of significance. Thus, each reading discloses some aspects of the work while it conceals others, each enables us to understand the text at one level while it limits us at another level.

In summarizing the various ways in which the meaning of *Utopia* has been inferred, Morson describes three major groupings or schools of readers (pp. 164–65). There is, first of all, a large group of readers who emphasize the irony and playfulness of More's text. For these readers, *Utopia* is primarily a political fantasy or a rhetorical exercise in wit and playful paradox. C. S. Lewis, for example, understood *Utopia* as "a holiday work, a spontaneous overflow of intellectual high spirits, a revel of debate, paradox, comedy and (above all) of invention, which starts many hares and kills none."[3] Understood this way, *Utopia* is "a jolly invention," as Lewis described it, which is apolitical in its orientation and playfully satirizes all concepts of ideal states or perfect communities.

A second school of readers emphasizes the social and political reforms advocated in More's text. For these readers, *Utopia* is a serious indictment of a corrupt and sinful social order and an effort to inspire social reform. These readers often focus their readings on More's humanism and his socialist ideals. Robert Adams, for example, finds that "More meant the *Utopia* . . . almost as seriously as he meant his resistance to Henry VIII."[4] Seen this way, More's text is grasped as a genuine sociopolitical critique that makes specific proposals intended for enactment.

A third group of readers, among whom Morson includes himself, emphasizes the inconclusiveness of both "playful" and "serious" readings and urges us to consider *Utopia* as an open-ended text, or, as Morson puts it, a "textually uncertain" meta-utopia (p. 164). Such readers acknowledge both the ironic playfulness and the serious intent of *Utopia*, but instead of limiting the significance of the text to one or the other they ask us to consider both as valid possibilities. This approach to reading *Utopia* either stresses the dialogue form and its enigmatic, open ending, or, like Morson, argues that each reading is dependent on the generic conventions and traditions according to which More's text is read. Morson observes that "those who read the work as a utopia take Hythloday as the delineator and class it with the *Republic* . . . and *Looking Backward*. When interpreted as a play of pure wit, *Utopia* is compared to Lucian's *True History*" (p. 173). In allowing for the possibility of both "playful" and "serious" readings, one regards *Utopia* as an open text that does not reconcile all contradictions and dissolve all dichotomies but rather implicates the reader in a contradictory game—a dialectical process that makes conflicting demands and leaves the reader with numerous discrepancies and discontinuities to resolve for himself.

To illustrate the benefits of reading *Utopia* as an open and inconclusive play of contraries, I would like to consider, in some detail, Louis Marin's provocative reading. In *Utopiques: Jeux d'espaces* (1973) and in his essay "Toward a Semiotic of Utopia: Political and Fictional Discourse in Thomas More's *Utopia*" (1978), Marin provides a semiotic-structural analysis of utopian narrative and delineates a method of reading More's text that unlocks some surprising potentialities. Marin's method of "decoding" *Utopia* locates the functions and effects of More's text in its contradictions and its incongruities— features which bring the reader more dynamically into play and which can make the act of reading *Utopia* a more productive experience.

Marin's basic premises are summarized in a brief and central chapter in *Utopiques* entitled "Theses on Ideology and Utopia."[5] Here Marin argues that a utopia is not a representation of a perfect version of the author's society but rather a "displaced" or dislocated version projected into a fictive no-time or no-place. In this displacement, Marin observes, utopias suspend sociopolitical analysis and shift from argument and dialogue to narrative description. This shift from analysis to fiction is crucial for Marin. It constitutes the essential characteristic of all "utopian practice": the juxtaposition of a fictive permutation against a familiar reality. As fictions, utopias symbolically transform existing society and are therefore "fantastically exterior to that society, history, ideology" (p. 72). For Marin, then, utopia is truly "the *other* of real society" (p. 72); it displaces concrete social and historical analysis with utopian vision. The process of constructing this vision involves a form of preconceptual thinking—a form of wish-dreaming—that lacks "critical awareness" of itself. Hence, for Marin, utopia constitutes a "critical preface" to the more theoretical and conceptual analysis provided by Marxism. Marin's first thesis is that "utopia is an ideological critique of the dominant ideology" (p. 71); that is, utopia negates existing values and institutions but its negativity "remains fictive." Without a theory or concept to account for historical change, utopias remain prelogical and unscientific, unable to provide a method for understanding and changing the nature of social relations.

The fictive status of all utopias is the basis of Marin's second thesis, which argues that utopia is "*figuratively* the *other* or negative of contemporary social reality" (p. 72). In Marin's view, utopia "is not a place located outside space, or imaginary, or unreal, but rather the not-place, the place without determination, the very figure of the neuter" (p. 72). As an indeterminate no-place, utopia is literally nowhere, a neutral "space" between opposites. Our task in reading utopias, according to Marin, is to fill in this space or indeterminate area, that is, to reconstruct the underlying social and political conflicts which the utopian figure inverts and neutralizes. Marin's method of reading utopias, as we shall see shortly, requires that we read the utopian text against itself in order to produce "a structure of divergencies within the figurative product, and of a topological mapping of the play of the various signifying and signified spaces in the figure" (p. 73). This method allows Marin to uncover numerous contradictions and inconsistencies in the social, economic, and political fabric of the utopian "figure."

Marin's third thesis invests utopias with a limited anticipatory power. "Utopian discourse," he states, "is the one form of ideological discourse that has an anticipatory value of a theoretical kind: but it is a value which can only appear as such when theory has itself been elaborated, that is to say, subsequent to the emergence of the material conditions for new productive forces" (p. 75). In other words, for Marin, the "anticipatory value" of utopias can be discerned only after scientific theory has arrived on the historical scene, an arrival which, however, also spells the end of utopia. Marin argues that this anticipatory function ends with the arrival of Marxism, an event which makes utopias obsolete. Even though post-Marxist utopias continue to be written, for Marin these utopias lack the critical anticipatory value that he finds in pre-nineteenth-century models.[6]

On the basis of these theses, Marin provides a rather elaborate method for reading utopias. Essentially, this method requires that we discard the notion of utopia as a detailed rendering of an ideal society and regard it instead as a "play" of opposites that intimates an alternative future, a future of which the utopian author is only vaguely aware. Limited by historical circumstances, the author strains to project an alternative to existing society; this fictive construction, however, remains inarticulate, fragmented, and confused, the result of figurative thinking or wishful dreaming. But when subjected to critical scrutiny, this utopian figure can be seen to both reveal and conceal the social changes which, in the author's own time, cannot be expressed conceptually but only indicated symbolically. Marin's approach may seem idiosyncratic, but its substance becomes apparent when he applies his premises to texts. His reading of More's *Utopia* is exemplary, for in applying his premises Marin uncovers some surprising contradictions in More's text.

Marin begins his analysis of *Utopia* by emphasizing the indeterminacy of More's fictive island, which can be understood as "nowhere" or as "a place of happiness." Marin reads it literally as "happiness in indeterminacy." This play on words suggests, Marin argues, that More's text is best thought of as a "play on spaces," the central function of which is to map out political, social, and economic "spaces" which constitute a "picture" drawn up by More to defamiliarize the deficiencies that exist in his own social environment. For Marin, the critical impact of *Utopia* lies in the differences that distinguish this utopian "picture" from its historical reality. These differences, Marin notes, are most evident in the shift that occurs from Book I to Book II of *Utopia*—a shift from critical analysis of the social problems afflicting England in 1516 to Hythloday's description of a fictive island. For Marin, the utopian method is best defined by this shift in which political argument is displaced by utopian fiction. In More's text this shift occurs when "More" and Hythloday break off their argument and Hythloday proceeds to sketch out a verbal picture of life among the Utopians, who have ostensibly resolved all conflict, mediated all oppositions, and reconciled all contradictions.

Marin finds, however, that these resolutions are not accomplished in the text. Hythloday's description of no-place is in various ways incongruous in structure and function; that is, it does not reconcile the political discrepancies uncovered by critical analysis but rather "neutralizes" them by projecting them into a fictive space. In More's text this projection is a new island that is neither Old World nor New World, neither Europe nor America, but some neutral and indeterminate place in between. Marin points out that the opposition between money and poverty, which political analysis reveals to be the reason for the social conflict in 1516 England, is not reconciled but "neutralized" in Utopia, where citizens are neither rich nor poor. Even the names within Utopia, Marin reminds us, suggest this kind of neutralization: there is a river whose name means "no-water" (Anydrus), a prince whose name means "no-people" (Ademus), and, of course, "Utopia" itself, which means "no-place."

If we now read Book II of *Utopia* as a "displacement" and "neutralization" of the problems uncovered in Book I, we should discover inconsistencies and incongruities that would make the utopian island something less or something "other" than a perfect version of historical England of 1516. And, indeed, Marin finds numerous discrepancies in Hythloday's account of the political and economic organization of the Utopian city. Each city, Hythloday informs us, is divided into a network of blocks, streets, and districts: each block has at its center a common garden; each street constitutes a political entity of thirty families who share a communal dining hall; each district constitutes an economic unit with a market at its center. Hythloday informs us that food grown in the block's garden is taken to the district marketplace and then consumed in the street's common dining hall. Marin observes, however, that this network of relations in effect transforms a block's product into commodities at the district level; these commodities are then consumed at the street level, where the food was grown in the first place. Given Hythloday's account that the Utopians have eliminated all money, there should be "no-place" for a market in his description of the economic organization of Utopia.

A similar inconsistency, Marin notes, can be seen in the political organization of Utopia, which, we are told, consists in a federation of equal states. Indeed, complete equality is the foundation stone of Utopian institutions and practice. And yet, Hythloday informs us that there is a capital, Amaurotum, and a prince, Ademus. Strictly speaking, there should be "no-place" for either in the political organization of Utopia.

Marin reads these seemingly minor inconsistencies as indices of deeper historical contradictions existing in the social and political developments of More's own time. Through these barely noticeable discrepancies Marin finds that "More's discourse reveals the ideology of the ascending class, the bourgeoisie in the first step of its development."[7] This historical development is evidenced further, according to Marin, in such Utopian activities as carrying on a flourishing trade with neighboring countries, launching colonial wars abroad, and hiring mercenaries to fight in these wars. Marin's point is that all the historical signs necessary for our understanding of the role of money in a central marketplace and the centralization of power in the state (the prince) in an emerging capitalist society are present in *Utopia,* but they are "prefigured" or perceived on a preconceptual level, in the absence of a social theory that could explain and demystify the real role of money and power in a capitalist society. Thus, for Marin, Hythloday's description of Utopia provides the reader with a "neutral space" where the historical contradictions of 1516 England are distanced and made more accessible—not reconciled or resolved. As an "ideological critique of the dominant ideology," the power of Utopia lies in this process of defamiliarization.

A more dramatic example of the kinds of incongruities and inconsistencies that Marin uncovers in *Utopia* is provided by his analysis of the dialogue in Book I on counseling princes. Here, it will be recalled, "More," Giles, and Hythloday debate about various social problems that afflict their society: poverty, crime, lack of social justice, war, the effects of the enclosure movement. "More" and Giles argue for social reforms brought about by giving rational advice to princes; Hythloday insists that such reforms are mere palliatives and argues that only the complete elimination of money and private property can bring about a just society. In the ensuing discussion, Hythloday recounts a debate that he had at John Morton's house, a debate on the question of whether the death penalty is an appropriate punishment for theft. Hythloday's argument against capital punishment, Marin notes, is based on two separate and inconsistent kinds of analysis: the first one is religious and ethical in nature ("Thou shalt not kill"); the second is based on economic and political analysis. In his economic analysis, Hythloday, by showing how the forces of inflation and centralization of power have produced a situation in which feudal lords are forced to disband their armies, demonstrates quite effectively how the breakdown of the feudal system has disrupted social stability. These armies, now unemployed, are left to roam the countryside as "a vast multitude of such people as trouble and disturb the peace."[8] In a similar way, the enclosure movement has uprooted a large number of unemployed peasants—history's first example of a surplus population—who, without a means of livelihood, are forced into towns where they resort to theft in order to survive: "And what, I ask, have they to do but to beg, or—a course more readily embraced by men of mettle—to become robbers?" (p. 27).

Marin notes that this argument is a lucid critique of the sociopolitical effects of rising capitalism but also observes that it "is disconnected from the theological assumptions according to which 'Human life cannot be equivalent to money,' private property cannot balance human life" (p. 272). This inconsistency, Marin points out, is due to the transitional period in history from which vantage Hythloday/More is unable to conceive of a genuine alternative to either feudalism or capitalism. Consequently, Hythloday/More shifts from historical analysis of existing problems to utopian fiction, or, as Marin puts it, "producing a utopian representation in the middle of political argumentation" (p. 272). This "utopian representation" attempts to bridge the gap, to provide "the missing link between the theological thesis and the social and economic analysis" (p. 273). The "missing link" takes the form of a utopian figuration which tries to articulate this inconsistency in the absence of a political theory that could explain it. In other words, Hythloday's analysis expresses rather than reconciles the contradictions between a fading feudal system based on ethical relationships and the new social relations, based on money relationships, emerging under capitalism. But, in Marin's view, Hythloday only succeeds in vaguely anticipating the new form of social relations.

The "missing link" that Hythloday provides in his argument against capital punishment is the "micro-utopia" of the Polylerites. Among these fictive people Hythloday claims to have discovered the "proof" for his argument. In this well-governed nation, "the object of public anger is to destroy the vices but save the persons" (p. 33). Instead of imposing the death penalty for theft, the Polylerites have devised various ways in which the criminal is able to make restitution to the victim. Hythloday explains in detail how thieves among these exemplary people are dressed identically, forced to wear special badges, and further identified by cutting off the tips of their ears. But the real problem in this elaborate utopian "proof," as Marin points out, is that it is irrelevant to the question of legal punishment for theft. By Hythloday's own account, Marin observes, theft should not occur within this utopian society: "No misery means no larceny. But, in fact, there are thieves in this utopia. How is this possible since that country knows neither misery nor unemployment?" (p. 275). Again, Marin reads this glaring contradiction as a symptom of deeper historical developments occurring within More's society. Since these criminals among the Polylerites are forced to work continuously and wear uniforms and are paid wages, they become, in Marin's reading, "interchangeable parts" in society and prefigure "the concept of commodity as applied to labor . . . the selling of labor power for a salary" (pp. 275–76). In other words, these thieves who have "no-place" in Utopia anticipate their social counterparts, the proletarian workers, in a rising capitalist economy. For Marin, then, the critical power and value of these displaced and inverted utopian images lies in their capacity to reveal significant historical processes even though the authors of these images may be blind to this value.

Marin's reading of this kind of significance into minor details of More's work may appear to be anachronistic and may seem to "read too much" into the text. Nevertheless, his approach is productive because it allows us to understand More's *Utopia* "not as an inert model that mechanistically inverts the negative relations of reality into positive ones" (p. 276), but rather as a "figurative anticipation . . . that conceals and reveals the self-cleavage of social reality" (p. 279). Instead of understanding More's text as a dreamlike solution that reconciles all conflicts and antagonisms, we can now grasp it as a provisional, fragmentary, and contradictory construction whose efficacy lies in the process of transvaluation and in its playful distancing of prevailing social forms. Read this way, More's *Utopia* can be an activating experience in which the reader makes his own discoveries. As a "work of figuration," More's text can be seen to have effects comparable to those of a symbol. Like a symbol, More's fictive no-place is both denotative and connotative; it presents a world that is similar but not identical to the world of its composition. The similarities establish a contiguous relationship with the author's society; the differences invest it with a metaphorical or revelatory power. Marin shows how the two levels of discourse that produce this symbol—the historical-political analysis of what "is" and the utopian projection of what "ought" to be—dialectically converge in such a way as to indicate and illuminate deep-seated historical contradictions.

Thus, for Marin, More's *Utopia* is not a blueprint that formulates unambiguous answers for social problems, nor is it an exercise in pure wit: rather, its efficacy is in heightening the reader's awareness of the incongruities between social fact and utopian vision and in making him more conscious of the contradictions that exist within the author's society. Read this way, *Utopia* no longer appears to be a static synthesis, a vision of a tranquil paradise, that reconciles all oppositions and contraries. When interrogated more carefully, this apparent synthesis reveals and intensifies numerous gaps and inconsistencies in the political-historical-economic structure of society. In filling in these gaps, the reader becomes the strategic site at which the political and fictional forms of discourse converge.

It is, however, not absolutely necessary that we subject More's text to such subtle scrutiny in order to locate contradictions and discrepancies within the structure and organization of More's no-place. Indeed, very few readers have found Utopia to be a perfect version of More's own society, and some have claimed that it is considerably less than a good-place. More's procedure in constructing "the best state of a commonwealth" is more aptly described in Book I when "More" admonishes Hythloday: "What you cannot turn to good you must make as little bad as you can. For it is impossible that all should be well unless all men were good, a situation which I do not expect for a great many years to come" (p. 50). But even this more limited objective has been questioned from time to time. Bertrand Russell, for example, found that "life in More's Utopia . . . would be intolerably dull. Diversity is essential to happiness, and in Utopia there is hardly any. This is a defect of all planned social systems, actual as well as imaginary."[9] Other readers have found that life in More's fictive community would be not only dull but severely restrictive of human possibilities. These readers have observed that Utopia is coercive, dogmatic, male-dominated, puritanical, primed for war, and imperialistic. It seems, then, that in terms of its effects on readers, More's description of Utopia actually has very little in common with an image of perfect happiness and timeless tranquility. What strikes us instead are the contradictions and deficiencies that characterize the social, economic, and political institutions that More describes. These deficiencies constitute a "defect" in More's vision only so long as we evaluate More's text as a depiction of perfect social relations—as Bertrand Russell apparently did. They take on a different significance if we focus our attention on the effects that these contradictions can have on readers.

The contradictions that remain within the borders of More's projected no-place become more apparent when we remember that its most radical feature is the elimination of possessions and competition through common ownership of all goods. Hythloday, like his mentor Plato, insists that "the one and only road to the general welfare lies in the maintenance of equality in all respects" (p. 53). And yet, if we look more carefully at the exposition of life within Utopia, we find a hierarchical social structure based on the complete authority of the elders. We are informed, for example, that the elders dominate the educational system, that they exercise control over politics and religion, and that they oversee all social activities to the point of receiving privileged seating and treatment in the communal dining halls. Further, we are told that scholars in Utopia are "given perpetual freedom from labor through the secret vote of the syphogrants so they may learn thoroughly the various branches of knowledge" (p. 73), and that priests and public officials are singled out for special regard. The Utopian ideal of complete equality is apparently not extended to women, either, since Hythloday reports that "wives wait on their husbands, children on their parents, and generally the younger on their elders" (p. 77). Once a month, wives kneel before their husbands, admit their shortcomings, and beg for forgiveness. Worse yet, in this ostensibly classless society there are "classes of slaves" whom the Utopians "keep not only continually at work but also in chains" (p. 108). One such class of slaves consists of disinherited persons who come to Utopia looking for a better life, "for sometimes a hard-working and poverty-stricken drudge of another country voluntarily chooses slavery in Utopia" (p. 108). The reader is puzzled as to why these poor individuals are treated this way and why they are described as "poverty-stricken" in a society that has abolished money and property.

The Utopian premise of "equality in all respects" is further contradicted when Hythloday reports that Utopians compete in producing the best gardens. Given the ideal of equality, there should be no competition and certainly no private gardens in a society where no one owns anything. Also, this Utopian ideal does not extend beyond Utopia's borders, since Utopians own property in other countries from which they collect large sums of money to finance wars. Further, it is apparent that Hythloday's eloquent argument against capital punishment and in favor of the system of retribution that prevails among the Polylerites is rejected in Utopia, where the death penalty is imposed on those found guilty of a second offense of adultery and on slaves who "rebel and kick against" their condition. The latter "are thereupon put to death like untameable beasts that cannot be restrained by prison or chain" (p. 112). And finally, in religious matters Hythloday reports that King Utopus "made the whole matter of religion an open question and left each one free to choose what he should believe" (p. 134). But this principle of tolerance is contradicted in the next sentence, which tells us that Utopus "conscientiously and strictly gave injunction that no one should fall so far below the dignity of human nature as to believe that souls likewise perish with the body or that the world is mere sport of chance and not governed by any divine providence" (p. 134). Although not explicitly punished, these materialists and atheists are not counted as citizens, have no civil rights, and are publicly ostracized.

Rather than providing us with a resolution of social problems, More's *Utopia* actually presents us with numerous contradictions. The utopian effort to reconcile all oppositions ends up, paradoxically, producing its own; in its desire to dissolve all discrepancies, *Utopia* makes us more conscious of them; in seeking to establish itself outside its own time and place, it brings us into closer contact with both; in presenting itself as a static construction that is beyond change and contingency, *Utopia* demonstrates the inevitability of social change and even arouses our desire for it. These paradoxes indicate that the reader's role in *Utopia* cannot be to passively accept Utopian formulations as superior in all respects but rather to respond more critically and more actively in determining what these formulations exclude or repress. In uncovering the contradictions and deficiencies that remain within the boundaries of Utopia, the reader is brought more dynamically into play. Her task now is to subject Utopia itself to a process of critical distancing that will reveal Utopia's own limits and shortcomings. What becomes more apparent in this method of reading More's *Utopia* is a basic duplicity in the text's strategy: what seems like a retreat from social reality, an image of perfect harmony and closure, becomes an effort to arouse the reader and bring her into closer touch with social reality, which is now revealed as provisional, contradictory, and open-ended.

In view of the structural inconsistencies and the contradictions in More's text, it is not surprising that readers have reached divergent conclusions about its meaning. *Utopia* can be deciphered at different levels as an idle fantasy, a play of wit, a scholar's dream, a social satire, a blueprint for a better society, and a subversive political philosophy. Each of these readings unlocks some significance in the text, but none is determinate, exhaustive, or objectively true. One reason for this, as Marin's deconstructive reading shows, is that More's text consists of incongruent and heterogeneous forms of fictional and political discourse; different readers link these forms of discourse in different ways and emphasize one at the expense of the other.

Another, perhaps more apparent, reason is the open-endedness of the dialogue, which leaves the reader suspended between two unreconciled perspectives on Utopian values. These two perspectives are represented in the text by the voices of Hythloday and "More," who provide the reader with conflicting pro- and anti-utopian arguments. Hythloday argues for revolutionary utopian changes; "More," who may or may not represent More's own views, argues for gradual reform. This provides the reader with two perspectives— each of which is deficient when viewed from the other. From the point of view of "More," Hythloday's radical arguments appear extreme, uncompromising, and potentially dangerous. Hence, "More" cautions us against Hythloday's intran-

93

sigence and Manichean outlook. From Hythloday's point of view, "More's" cautionary arguments conceal an attitude of appeasement and a readiness to compromise revolutionary demands for superficial reforms. Each point of view can be persuasive, and, since neither wins the argument conclusively, the reader is put in a situation analogous to that of a juror in a courtroom: he listens to both arguments, considers both points of view, and draws his own conclusions.[10] It is true, of course, that Hythloday dominates the dialogue and that he gives the most forceful arguments, but we must recall that he is also, as his name indicates, an "expert in trifles" and "well learned in nonsense." "More's" function is to inject a note of skepticism and doubt about Hythloday's claims, thereby forcing the reader to assume a more critical attitude.

The arguments between "More" and Hythloday begin in Book I with a disagreement on whether it is possible to change society by working within the system (by providing wise counsel to a prince). "More" reflects a moderate position in his "indirect approach": "If you cannot pluck up wrong-headed opinions by the root, if you cannot cure according to your heart's desire vices of long standing, yet you must not on that account desert the commonwealth. You must not abandon the ship in a storm because you cannot control the winds, . . . you must not force upon people new and strange ideas which you realize will carry no weight with persons of opposite conviction. On the contrary, by the indirect approach you must seek and strive to the best of your power to handle matters tactfully" (p. 50). Hythloday, on the other hand, is opposed to all halfway measures and indirect approaches. He prefers a direct, either/or approach: either a radical break with the corrupt status quo or nothing. "By this approach," he replies abruptly, "I should accomplish nothing else than to share the madness of others as I tried to cure their lunacy. If I would stick to the truth, I must needs speak in the manner I have described. To speak falsehoods, for all I know, may be the part of a philosopher, but it is certainly not for me" (p. 50).

On one point Hythloday's position is intransigent: "It appears to me," he states, "that wherever you have private property and all men measure all things by cash values, there it is scarcely possible for a commonwealth to have justice or prosperity" (p. 52). Hythloday's function is to argue the case that only the abolition of private property can lead to happiness; the function of "More" is to cast doubt on this premise by asking pertinent questions: "Life cannot be satisfactory where all things are in common. How can there be a sufficient supply of goods when each withdraws himself from the labor of production? For the individual does not have the motive of personal gain and he is rendered slothful by trusting to the industry of others" (p. 55). Hythloday goes on to argue that Utopia is an accomplished fact, not just a possibility. But "More's" skepticism has indicated that Hythloday's dogmatic claims and assertions ought to be disputed and questioned. Hythloday's views should be scrutinized from the perspective of "More," just as "More's" counterarguments depend on Hythloday's "proof." Implicit in this dialectic, the reader constitutes the site at which these arguments converge. In this pivotal role, the reader is able to entertain "the new island of Utopia" as a provisional and hypothetical construct intended to present "the best state of a commonwealth" at the same time that he remains skeptical and doubtful of many of its features.

It is this kind of dialectical disputation between utopian and nonutopian approaches that constitutes the central strategy of all utopian discourse. The effect of this strategy is to heighten our perception of contrasts through a dialectical structure that inverts standards and values to defamiliarize them. Thus, later in his exposition of life on this new island, Hythloday informs us that gold and silver are used as chamber pots, as toys for children, and as fetters to bind prisoners. But since gold and silver are ill-suited for these functions, the point is clearly to defamiliarize and dramatize their uses in More's own society. It is precisely the absurd and contradictory uses of gold and silver in Utopia that reinforce this effect.

Rather than constituting a flawed text that is inconsistent and paradoxical, More's *Utopia* can thus be read as an effort to stimulate and provoke the reader through numerous inversions and contradictions. Approached in this way, the limitations usually attributed to More's text—its reductiveness, its arrogant claims and assertions, its "impure" mixture of political and fictional forms of discourse, its numerous unresolved arguments and contradictions—can be seen as its most productive features. These characteristics of *Utopia* produce that creative interplay between reader and text that forces the reader to try to fill in the gaps between social fact and utopian fiction and to resolve the contradictions that the text produces. It is the suggestiveness of More's *Utopia*, its constant appeal to the reader to entertain oppositions, paradoxes, and contraries, that makes it "a startlingly subversive idea."[11] *Utopia* is subversive in the best sense of the word: it undermines the complacencies of habit and routine and challenges the reader with inconclusive contradictions which only his active mental and imaginative participation can begin to resolve. The effect of reading More's *Utopia* is ambivalent and dynamic even if the no-place itself is static. In reading *Utopia* we should, like "More," remain skeptical: "When Raphael had finished his story, many things came to my mind which seemed absurdly established in the customs and laws of the people described—not only in their method of waging war, their ceremonies and religion, as well as their other institutions, but most of all in that feature which is the principal foundation of their whole structure. I mean their common life and subsistence—without any exchange of money" (p. 151).

But we should also, like "More," be ready to entertain utopian possibilities more eagerly, looking for "another chance to think about these matters more deeply, and to talk them over . . . more fully" (p. 152). This approach will test our own capacities to envision Utopia and take us to the limits that the logic of contradictions will allow.

5

The Anti-Utopia
The Necessity of History

Revolutions are infinite. . . . We know for the time being there is no final number.

— YEVGENY ZAMYATIN, *We*, TRANS. MIRRA GINSBURG

One person's utopian dream turns out to be another's nightmare. It is not entirely unexpected, therefore, that ventures into utopia have aroused various forms of opposition and dissent. Plato's *Republic*, it will be recalled, spurred the counterarguments of Aristotle; More's *Utopia* inspired numerous parodies and imitations; Bellamy's *Looking Backward* provoked a number of critical rejoinders. These dissenting voices often responded by devising their own "ideal commonwealth," and in the process they raised fundamental questions about utopian thought and identified many of its deficiencies and limitations. In general, these opposing voices have questioned utopian claims to absolute truth and certainty and rejected the utopian faith in reason, universal happiness, and inevitable progress. Marx and Engels summarized these arguments against utopia in their polemical attacks on the nineteenth-century "utopian socialists" Fourier, Owen, and Saint-Simon. In his essay "Socialism: Utopian and Scientific," Engels criticized these utopian thinkers for their failure to provide a concrete method to implement their visions. The danger of all utopian thought, according to Engels, is that it represents a diversion of revolutionary energies into fantasies and imaginary satisfactions, a form of escapism that denies the reality of history.[1] It is precisely in their timelessness and in their failure to take into account the dynamics of history that utopias have proven most vulnerable to anti-utopian attacks.

Yet the founders of Marxism remained sympathetic toward utopian goals. They considered the "utopian socialists" important forerunners of their own "scientific" form of socialism and appropriated many utopian features for it. In their criticism they urged correction and modification of utopian methods and strategies rather than outright rejection of utopian ends. The true enemies of utopia, or the real anti-utopians, it seems, did not emerge until the mid-twentieth century, when opposition to all forms of utopianism became far more hostile and one-dimensional. With the exception of the short-lived utopianism of the 1960s, utopia has become synonymous with totalitarianism, the complete antithesis of the "open society." What was once perceived as a promise of a rich and rewarding collective life, based on peace, community, and cooperation, has come to be seen as a dangerous repression of freedom, a denial of individuality, and a loss of conscious life altogether. In short, utopia has become anathema, a nightmare of political repression and total uniformity to be avoided at all costs. This dramatic shift in meaning constitutes a remarkable semantic inversion. Robert Elliott sums up this shift in meaning when he observes that "utopia is a bad word today not because we despair of being able to achieve it but because we fear it. Utopia itself . . . has become the enemy."[2]

Those who have tried to account for this reversal in meaning have turned to recent history. Elliott notes, for example, that utopia has always implied a faith in progress and a conviction that human beings can to some extent rationally shape their own social life. Today, such a faith is hard to sustain in view of historical developments. After two world wars, Hiroshima,

Auschwitz, and Vietnam, any talk of utopian possibilities seems somewhat absurd. For many people today, any hope of utopia after Hitler and Stalin is pure folly. Others have argued that the failure of socialism in the Soviet Union, once thought to be a model utopian experiment, and the failures of numerous smaller utopian experiments in the forms of religious and secular communes, is sufficient evidence that utopianism is not only ineffective but untenable. Still others have traced the decline of utopian values to the emergence of consumer capitalism in the West and monopoly socialism in the East. These developments, they argue, have produced political situations in which inertia, complacency, and a general satisfaction with things as they are have repressed the desire to contemplate any kind of significant social change. In the 1960s and 1970s, Herbert Marcuse diagnosed the various ways in which both capitalist and socialist societies deny the utopian imagination. This repression, Marcuse warned, could result in the total atrophy of the utopian impulse and consequently produce a "one-dimensional" society in which even the memory of a utopian dream sinks into total oblivion.[3]

However we ultimately account for the dialectical inversion of the meaning of utopia and for the general decline of the utopian imagination in our time, we must acknowledge a corresponding rise and proliferation of anti-utopian values and attitudes. Utopia's "fall from grace," as Elliott puts it, becomes evident enough when we consider the immense readership and influence of Bellamy's *Looking Backward*, which sold millions of copies and was translated into more than twenty languages after its publication in 1887.[4] There have been no literary utopias with a comparable impact since then. What we have instead is a variety of vivid anti-utopian visions that depict ever-bleaker possibilities: the effects of nuclear war, biological conditioning, pollution, automation, technocracy, and so on. These apocalyptic visions and the shift in social values that they entail are so pervasive that they dominate our cultural life. Anti-utopian sentiments can be detected in cultural expressions ranging from science fiction to existentialist philosophy; they are evident in popular films, in television programs, and in the products of mass culture generally.

The distinct shift in social values becomes apparent when we compare the typical hero (or anti-hero) in these anti-utopian works with the typical hero of utopian fiction. In stark contrast to the ingenuous utopian visitor who discovers that self-realization lies in human fellowship and in commitment to community, the hero in anti-utopian works is usually pitted against society, family, or social group. Self-realization is a possibility that exists only in breaking away from a corrupt and deforming social order. Authentic existence is available only for the outsider, on an individual level, not within society, within social relations, or on the level of working with others. This valorization of the individual and his freedom to choose—even if his choice is antisocial and self-destructive—reveals a basic distrust of all social groups. The latter are usually presented as distractions in which the individual loses himself in order to evade his existential condition. (At the same time, however, some anti-utopias, such as Zamyatin's *We*, indicate that this rejection of family, community, and social group also entails a significant loss. This loss is made evident, as we shall see, in the hero's gnawing sense of alienation, separation, and fragmentation.)

This valorization of the uprooted individual who struggles against a dehumanizing community is the central concern of those explicitly anti-utopian works which, on the surface at least, seem so intent on discrediting all utopian efforts. These anti-utopias or dystopias, of which *We, Brave New World,* and *Nineteen Eighty-Four* are the best-known examples, proceed by dialectically inverting utopian values so that the utopian hope

101

emerges as an object of fear or ambivalence.[5] Because of this critical inversion, we tend to think of these works as completely antithetical to the utopian impulse. On the ideological level, anti-utopias are seen as openly antagonistic toward all forms of socialism and communism. For Fredric Jameson, they represent an "unambiguous political position": he finds that "Utopia is a transparent synonym for socialism itself, and the enemies of Utopia sooner or later turn out to be the enemies of socialism."[6] This view is shared by Jean Pfaelzer, who writes that "dystopian fiction is formally and historically, structurally and contextually, a conservative genre."[7] Seen as politically reactionary texts, anti-utopias seem to discredit not only the utopian hope for progress but also the desirability of any kind of social change.

This kind of total inversion is also found on the formal level, where ideal utopian solutions are turned upside down and become nightmare possibilities. Morson, for example, who prefers anti-utopias to utopias, argues that anti-utopia is a "parodic genre" that exposes the deceptions and false assumptions of utopias, thereby depriving them of their potential impact on readers. His essential distinction is that "utopias describe an escape *from* history," whereas "anti-utopias describe an attempted escape *to* history, which is to say, the world of contingency, conflict, and uncertainty" (p. 128). Thus, for Morson, anti-utopia constitutes "the rebirth of the novel" on the formal level, since it reintroduces the possibility of conflict, doubt, anxiety, and tragedy into its fictive projection.

These distinctions are, of course, helpful in defining two opposing political stances and two distinct views of history and human happiness. But in drawing up these boundaries so rigidly, we can lose sight of the similar effects of these forms on readers. Both utopias and anti-utopias, after all, explore social possibilities theoretically; both move toward symbolism and allegory; and both set out to provoke the reader with contradictions and paradoxes that force him to entertain alternative values and alternative attitudes toward social problems. Even though utopias project a desirable world, while anti-utopias project a nightmare world, both make use of a dialectical structure that juxtaposes contradictory possibilities to create a cognitive tension between what is and what might be, a tension designed to induce a critical attitude toward the existing historical situation. Thus, anti-utopias, to the extent that they do not merely try to justify the status quo, are not so much the total antithesis of utopias as they are efforts to inspire the reader with the same concern and unrest that utopias inspire.

Rather than an antithesis of utopia, the anti-utopia is typically an inversion of utopia that plays on the same essential dialectical structure: we know what utopia is by knowing what it is not. A closer reading of most anti-utopias and an analysis of the reader activity they stimulate reveals that the text works to envision *indirectly* what utopia would be: a society that allows for personal fulfillment without the possibility of exploitation, that guarantees social harmony without becoming life-denying, that achieves order without suppressing spontaneity, and that secures stability without becoming hopelessly rigid. Seeing no resolution of social disparities, contradictions, and problems in the text, the reader is inspired to find it elsewhere—if only in the necessarily unfinished utopian dialogues of his own imagination. In short, anti-utopias compel the reader to the same dialogue, to the attempt to answer the same questions inspired by utopias.

Anti-utopias achieve their effects through satire and parody: they satirize existing social and technological tendencies by extrapolating and exaggerating the possible consequences of those tendencies, and they parody the utopian yearning for simple, timeless, and permanent solutions. Unlike utopias, which negate the existing system and then provide a negation of the negation—that is, a positive construction that

103

formulates a solution—anti-utopias may be seen as negations that do not undertake the task of reconstruction. In assuming an entirely negative position, they leave the act of construction up to the reader. Whereas utopias provide the reader with an image of hope, a positive figure that awakens desire for change, anti-utopias provide us with a negative figure, an image of hopelessness that arouses our fears and anxieties. But both utopias and anti-utopias express our deepest fantasies and fears about communal life, allowing us access to the constraints and contradictions that limit social possibilities. Their shared effects lie in their thought-provoking power, in their capacity to intensify contradictions and to arouse a desire for change. The enemy of both utopia and anti-utopia is the status quo, which both seek to transform.

Read this way, anti-utopias are not necessarily complete inversions that repudiate utopian ideology. Rather than subverting all utopian efforts and intentions, anti-utopias, more accurately, uncover problems, raise questions, and generate doubts about utopian claims, particularly the utopian claim to absolute certainty and timeless truth. Not unlike the Marxist critique of the "utopian socialists," anti-utopias tend to be more skeptical in exploring utopian assumptions. They delve more deeply into the historical conflicts and contradictions that utopias often dismiss, but they remain sympathetic to the utopian imperative for change and renovation. Where utopias seek to provide timeless and imaginary solutions, anti-utopias are more intent on interrogating and defamiliarizing these solutions in order to reveal their contradictory and paradoxical nature.

Most important, anti-utopias, like utopias, expose the myths and falsehoods upon which existing society is constructed. This occurs usually in a characteristic scene in which the key authority figure in anti-utopia—the Benefactor (*We*), Mustapha Mond (*Brave New World*), O'Brien (*Nineteen Eighty-Four*)—reveals to a rebellious hero the deception on which his

dominance and power are based. In this revelatory scene, the
nature of political and social arrangements is exposed as arbitrary and capricious, based either on a benevolent lie, as in
Brave New World and *We,* or on brutal distortions, as in
Nineteenth Eighty-Four. In either case, the reader is forced to recognize that social reality is provisional, a precarious and open-
ended project of which human beings are the authors. Anti-
utopias are disturbing because they forcefully remind us that
existing along with the possibility of the best of all possible
worlds is the possibility of a future that may be the worst of
all possible worlds. This recognition is the point of departure
for the kind of critical interrogation of utopian values that we
find in Zamyatin's *We,* an anti-utopia that relentlessly histor-
icizes the static oppositions of classical utopias, not in order
to repudiate them but in order to reveal their dialectical and
contradictory truths.

Among the many anti-utopias that project a closed, total-
itarian future, *We* deserves special consideration.[8] Like
More's *Utopia, We* has achieved the status of an exemplary
work whose influence can be seen in numerous imitations:
Huxley's *Brave New World,* Orwell's *Nineteen Eighty-Four,*
Golding's *Lord of the Flies,* Bradbury's *Fahrenheit 451,* Burgess's
Clockwork Orange, and many others. And like More's *Utopia,
We* nearly exhausts the possibilities of its genre. *We* is a multifaceted work that self-consciously explores the contradictory
relationship between utopian and anti-utopian alternatives in
order to provoke the reader with paradoxes. Rather than simply satirizing the narrowness of utopian ideals and endorsing
their opposites, Zamyatin provides the reader with a double
perspective that allows us to entertain both pro- and anti-utopian views and to become more aware of the limiting and
enabling features of each. The effect of this open-ended, dialectical structure is to enfold the reader in an inconclusive
thought-game in which antinomies and oppositions remain
unresolved, a process in which the ambiguities involved in

the question of what constitutes human happiness are interrogated rather than single-mindedly reduced.

This ambivalence toward utopian values serves to distinguish Zamyatin's work and others like it from the more genuine *dystopia*, or "bad-place," envisioned in such works as *Nineteen Eighty-Four*. Most readers have recognized that *Nineteen Eighty-Four* is not so much concerned with the question of human happiness as it is with projecting a fascist future dominated by a brutal and sadistic will to power.[9] Unlike the more or less beneficent rulers in *We* and *Brave New World*, who, as we shall see, take on the tragic dimensions of Dostoevsky's Grand Inquisitor, "The Party" in *Nineteen Eighty-Four* shows only contempt for its citizens, undermines human solidarity at every opportunity, and rules by the principles of "doublethink," mind control, and sheer terror. O'Brien, the ruler of this nightmare world, describes it as "the exact opposite of the stupid hedonistic Utopias that the old reformers imagined. A world of fear and treachery and torment, a world of trampling and being trampled upon. . . . Progress in our world will be progress toward more pain. The old civilizations claimed that they were founded on love and justice. Ours is founded on hatred."[10] By contrast, the societies depicted in *Brave New World* and *We* are not constructed on the motivation of destroying all utopian ideals. Indeed, the rulers of these future worlds are concerned about the well-being of their citizens and convinced that they have realized precisely that perfect happiness that "the old reformers" dreamed of. In *Brave New World* this realization takes the form of a thoroughly conditioned paradise in which happiness is reduced to a chemically induced feeling; in *We* it takes the form of an excessively rationalized and mechanized world in which happiness and freedom are found to be incompatible.

The incompatibility of happiness and freedom, as has often been noted, is the central issue in most anti-utopias. In *We* and *Brave New World* this opposition is presented in similar ways. Each work tells the story of a rebellion against utopian happiness, which is revealed as stultifying, repressive, and destructive of the values of choice, individuality, and change. Each work presents the reader with two dialectically opposed worlds separated by a boundary: on one side there is an extremely determined form of rationality, uniformity, order; on the other side there is extreme irrationality, wild profusion, disorder. The goal of the rebellion in both novels is to break down the barrier that separates these extremes—a barrier that can be read as a sign of alienation and fragmentation on both sides. In *Brave New World*, however, the dilemma between freedom and happiness is portrayed in a somewhat one-sided way: the wild profusion of nature outside the barrier is defended against the extremes of technology inside; individualistic values are given priority over social values. By radically inverting utopian values, *Brave New World* suggests that being unhappy is better than being happy, that the irrational is better than the rational, and that almost anything is better than utopian harmony. Thus, the rebellious Savage claims "the right to be unhappy." When Mustapha Mond reminds him that this entails "the right to grow old and ugly and impotent; the right to have syphilis and cancer; the right to have too little to eat; the right to be lousy; the right to live in constant apprehension of what may happen tomorrow; the right to catch typhoid; the right to be tortured by unspeakable pains of every kind," the Savage replies: "I claim them all."[11] For the passive reader at least, the novel's total inversion of utopian values limits the reader to choosing their opposites; one set of values cancels out the other, and the potential thought-provoking capacities of the anti-utopia are obviated.

In Zamyatin's *We*, however, the "correct" choice is not quite so apparent. Here the multiple oppositions between rationalism/irrationalism, science/art, stability/revolution, "We"/"I", Eros/love remain contradictory and open-ended. If we resolve these contradictions by aligning ourselves single-mindedly on one side or the other, we reproduce the kind of one-dimensional choice that the novel relentlessly criticizes. The paradoxes and contradictions the novel explores are more resonant and provocative precisely because the arguments for each side are left ambivalent—each containing the "truth" of the other position. The effect of this double perspective is to stimulate, or even to force, the reader to become more active in determining a possible resolution for these contradictions, a resolution beyond the boundaries of the oppositions represented in the text. The significance of *We* lies in its power to stimulate thought through a dialectical structure that intensifies contradictions rather than provides answers. In this sense, Zamyatin's novel is not so much anti-utopian as it is, in Zamyatin's own words, "antientropic," which is to say, against the status quo. Zamyatin himself characterized *We* as an example of "harmful literature," which he defined as "more useful than useful literature, for it is antientropic, it is a means of combating calcification, . . . it is utopian."[12] In contrast to *Nineteen Eighty-Four,* then, which depicts a world entirely devoid of utopian possibilities, and unlike *Brave New World* with its Manichean conclusions, *We* explores the irreconcilable tensions and contradictions implicit in all utopian efforts but leaves its readers free to draw their own conclusions. At the same time, however, Zamyatin's ambiguous anti-utopia forcefully cautions the reader that any potential conclusion she comes to must remain provisional, contingent, and inconclusive.

Zamyatin's text, like many anti-utopias, is set in a fictive future and describes life in a totalitarian state under the "benign yoke" of a "Benefactor." Within a completely glass-enclosed world, every aspect of life is carefully controlled and regulated: people are designated by numbers, all activity is subject to a "Table of Hours," everyone is visible in glass apartments. The explicit goal of this "United State" is "mathematically perfect happiness" (p. 1), which, in the context of the novel, entails the complete elimination of a sense of self and of all private experience. In the effort to achieve a totally rationalized and utilitarian way of life, science, ethics, and art alike have been reduced to mathematical equations: science celebrates rational equations and straight lines, "ethics is based on subtraction, addition, division, and multiplication" (p. 15), and the railway guide is considered to be "the greatest literary monument" (p. 12). Even sexual relations are spelled out in *Lex sexualis*, which proclaims that "each number has the right to any other number, as a sexual commodity" (p. 21). The "perfect happiness" that this society strives to attain entails the complete "crystallization of life," a "condition where nothing happens any more" (p. 24).

There are, however, some remaining obstacles that prevent the complete realization of this goal. From time to time, unruly Number-citizens rebel against this "perfect order." Some have even organized a small revolutionary group intent on destroying the "happiness" of the United State and creating a world of conflict, choice, and activity. This group calls itself "Mephi," and its members conspire, as the name suggests, to bring about another Fall in this inverted Garden of Eden. They plan their revolution from outside the Green Wall that encloses the United State and separates it from the chaotic and exuberant natural world of the revolutionaries. The goal of the revolution is to tear down this wall, to negate the existing system. The rebellion ultimately fails when the United State finds a way to remove the last obstacle to "perfect happiness"—an operation on the brain to "extirpate imagination," a lobotomy that guarantees perfect equilibrium at the cost of conscious life itself.

The narrator, D-503, who describes this atrophying world to us, is a mathematician and builder of the *Integral*, a rocket ship intended to spread the values of the United State to other planets. The diary that D-503 writes, which becomes the novel we read, is intended to celebrate the virtues of life

109

within the boundaries of the United State. In the process of describing his world, however, D-503 ironically reveals its repressive and dehumanizing features. And in the process of writing he gradually discovers himself, a "shaggy self" who is violent, erotic, and passionate beneath the surface of his rational social mask.

At the beginning of his manuscript, D-503 explains that the greatest achievement of his society is the elimination of individual personality. In the United State "nobody is 'one,' but 'one of'" (p. 7). But as his manuscript grows, so does his sense of an individual self, to the point where his "we" self is displaced by an "I" self. This "sickness," as it is diagnosed by a doctor, is compared to developing a "soul"—a sense of individual self-consciousness that is tantamount to treason in his "we"-dominated society. Initially this "sickness" takes the form of an erotic attraction to I-330, a female Number who is one of the leaders of the Mephi. Soon D-503 becomes aware of other irrational desires and illicit feelings: he begins to doubt the beneficence of his society and the certainties of his mathematics; he has erotic dreams (in a society where dreams are considered "a serious psychic disease" [p. 32]); he gradually develops a sense of subjective time; he experiences the intense exhilaration of violence; he realizes that he is capable of gratuitous and irrational thoughts and acts. These changes are rendered in subtle ways as D-503's perceptions of the world around him change: hard surfaces suddenly yield and become penetrable; habitual sounds and sights become disturbing and disorienting; glass and other fixed, shiny surfaces give way to unsettling fog, ambiguous clouds, threatening winds.

As his private self breaks free, D-503 experiences a dizzying sense of subjectivity: "I felt myself above all others. I was I, a separate entity, a world. I had ceased to be a component, as I had been, and become a unit" (p. 157). But D-503 interprets this liberating sense of freedom as a form of "madness." Unable to bear the terrible burden of this freedom, he readily submits to the operation that removes his imagination. In his final entry, after his operation, he indicates that he no longer recognizes or understands his own manuscript: "Can it be true that I, D-503, have written these two hundred pages? Can it really be true that I once felt—or imagined that I felt—all this?" (p. 231). D-503 has lost the ability to understand himself and the world he lives in. Docile and content, he has become a smoothly functioning cog in the social machine. But in spite of the terrifying finality of this conclusion, life in the United State has not yet congealed into total entropy. The revolution of the Mephi has failed, but part of the Green Wall has been torn down; thus the revolution has also, in part, succeeded. Given the powerful arguments in the novel for perpetual change and revolution, the reader can only expect new rebellions. The only constant acknowledged in the world of this novel is constant change.

Nevertheless, because of D-503's drastic solution to the freedom/happiness dilemma, our tendency is to read the novel as a devastating repudiation of utopian ideals and as a celebration of freedom. Morson, for example, finds that *We* teaches us important "counterlessons" which expose "not only the danger and folly of utopian lessons, but also the duplicitous strategies by which those lessons are taught" (p. 138). These counterlessons demonstrate the folly of trying to escape from history and reveal the dangers inherent in the utopian strategy of obscuring the boundary between fantasy and reality. Morson claims that anti-utopias generally re-establish this boundary by portraying the disastrous consequences of trying to realize utopian ideals. Other readers have read the novel as a powerful condemnation of the totalitarian tendencies inherent in all utopian thought. Gorman Beauchamp, for example, insists that "even the most benevolently intended utopias are, by the very nature of their claims, totalitarian, demanding the ultimate concern of their

111

subjects and asserting ultimate control over their destinies."[13] For Beauchamp, all utopias are based on "a systematic intensification of the restraints upon which all society rests" (p. 285), and all anti-utopias portray a rebellion against these constraints. In Beauchamp's reading, *We* is reduced to a one-sided representation of a revolt against the restraints of a totalitarian state. This revolt parallels the Christian myth of man's first fall from grace, his disobedience in the Garden of Eden. Like Adam, D-503 is seduced by Eve (I-330) into defying a godlike state by asserting his natural and instinctive drive for freedom. Beauchamp concludes that *We* discredits all utopian ideals and demonstrates the truth that freedom is more important than happiness, that instinct is more reliable than reason, that "I" is more valuable than "we": "Zamiatin's imagination has projected the ideal of utopian organization to its logical extreme" (p. 289) and found that individualism and instinctive freedom constitute "the essence of being human" (p. 292).

Clearly, these readings of Zamyatin's novel are conditioned by the value of personal freedom and reflect the prevailing anti-utopian attitudes of our time. What these readings fail to appreciate, it seems to me, are the ambiguities and unresolved ironies of the dialectical oppositions at work in Zamyatin's novel and their potentially ambivalent effects on the reader. These ambiguities are most evident in the complex imagery of the novel.

One such image is the Green Wall that insulates the "glass paradise" and seals it off from the "wild green ocean" outside. The wall is ironically described by D-503 as "the greatest of man's inventions":

> Man ceased to be a wild animal only when he built the first wall. Man ceased to be a savage only when we had built the Green Wall, when we had isolated our perfect mechanical world from the irrational, hideous world of trees, birds, animals. (P. 93)

This description reveals D-503's extreme alienation prior to the growth of his other self. Later, on the other side of the wall, he praises the opposite extreme, the liberating impact of extreme egotism: "Yes, yes, madness! And everyone must lose his mind, everyone must! The sooner the better! It is essential—I know it" (p. 158). In this way, *We* provides us with two extreme perspectives on the I/we dialectic. If we attempt to resolve this dialectic by reading the novel as an attack on the excessive rationalism inside the wall and a glorification of the excessive irrationalism outside the wall, we overlook the essential point of the wall, which is that it separates two equally disastrous forms of alienation.

The reader's task, then, is not to choose one form of alienation over another but to go beyond these two apparently irreconcilable opposites and attempt a possible mediation. Such a mediation implies the task of unbuilding walls, an effort to balance the opposing claims of "I" and "we," and a willingness to face contradictions honestly. Even though such mediations are identified by the poet R-13 as an impossible "third alternative" (p. 61), they are, in the context of the novel, the only alternative. As boundaries against uncertainty and the unknown, all walls prove illusory and temporary. *We* argues dramatically that no facet of human reality is ever complete, that history and biography constantly change, and that there are no final, conclusive answers. Even the Green Wall proves to be a temporary barrier because, as I-330 explains, "If the number of numbers is infinite, how can there be a final number? . . . [H]ow can there be a final revolution? There is no final one: revolutions are infinite. The final one is for children: children are frightened by infinity, and it's important that children sleep peacefully at night. . . . We know for the time being there is no final number" (pp. 174–75). At the same time, however, a world entirely without walls is also disastrous, as D-503's irrational praise of madness makes clear. At one point in the novel, when he encounters the "savages" outside, D-503 seems to realize that the wall separates two forms of alienation: "Who are they?" he asks, "the half we have lost? H_2 and O? And in order to get H_2O—streams, oceans, waterfalls, waves, storms—the two halves must unite" (p. 163).

Read this way, *We* becomes a more resonant text, one that provokes the reader with the extraordinary paradoxes that identify the utopian effort to balance and mediate contradictions. At one point I-330 explains that "there are two forces in the world—entropy and energy. One leads to blissful quietude, to happy equilibrium; the other, to destruction of equilibrium, to tormentingly endless movement" (p. 165). These two forces are presented as diametrically opposed; their coexistence constitutes an insoluble paradox. And yet, both are real and necessary even though each, by itself, leads to distortion and fragmentation. And though the novel sets them up as rigidly opposed, in the process of reading we are forced to rethink their contradictory significance and recognize the values of both.

Science and technology are presented to the reader in a similarly thought-provoking manner. Inside the wall, they are used as instruments for torture and repression; outside the wall they become a means of liberation. The spaceship *Integral*, for example, is intended to extend the ideological influence of the United State to other planets; but it can also be used to destroy that ideology. For the Mephi, the *Integral* becomes an instrument of change and rebellion. They intend to use it to tear down the wall and "to let the green wind blow from end to end—across the earth" (p. 157). To gain access to the *Integral*, I-330 manipulates D-503, turning him into a means to achieve the revolution's ends. For the Benefactor, on the other hand, the *Integral* is an instrument for constructing new walls, for carrying the values of the United State to other parts of the universe.

Similarly, the image of the knife indicates the paradoxical possibilities of technology. It is described by D-503 as "the

114

strongest, the most immortal, the most brilliant of man's creations. . . . [T]he knife is the universal means of solving all knots" (p. 117). This image is used by D-503 to justify the ethic of the United State—that the ends justify the means—but in the process he also indicates its paradoxical nature. The knife can be used by a surgeon or a highwayman: "Both may have the same knife in their hands, both do the same thing—cut a man's throat—yet one is a benefactor, the other a criminal; one has a + sign, the other a −" (p. 80). The knife, in other words, can be used to save human life, or it can be used to perform lobotomies. The paradox can be resolved only by decision and action, the uses we make of science and technology. As D-503 recognizes momentarily, "along the knife's edge is the road of paradoxes—the only road worthy of a fearless mind" (p. 117). This image suggests that the impossible "third alternative" is precisely "the road of paradoxes." This is a much more difficult road, but it avoids the pitfalls of a Manichean point of view and its single-minded conclusions. The challenge to the reader of Zamyatin's *We* is to construct a utopian alternative that responds to the demands of both self and community, a utopia that provides for freedom and happiness, stability and change, the rational and the irrational, security and history. It is an alternative not without contradictions, a genuine "no-place" that must be continually rethought.

The thought-provoking impact of *We* lies in these ambivalent images which disclose contradictory truths. *We* demonstrates that both excessive utopianism and excessive individualism can be regressive and crippling; D-503 struggles to free himself from one-sided determination by "we," but in the end it is one-sided determination by "I" that leads to his fateful decision. The deeper issue raised by his action is whether it makes any sense to champion one against the other, whether it is possible to be an "I" without a "we." To be meaningful, both individualism and utopianism must be placed in a historical context, and this context is contingent and always changing. Any effort to escape history only demonstrates its determining power, and any effort to deny the importance of the social community only leads to the ironic and relentless confirmation of its importance. Thus, *We* is not so much an attempt to discredit utopian values and champion individualism as it is an examination of the assumptions and logic underlying both pro- and anti-utopian arguments—an examination that forces the reader to assume a more critical and skeptical attitude toward both. For just as every utopia contains within it, explicitly or implicitly, an anti-utopia that it tries to transform, so every anti-utopia implies a utopian alternative, the construction of which is left up to the reader.

The pivotal scene in which the contradictory logic of utopias is made apparent occurs in that familiar confrontation between the ruler of anti-utopia and the rebellious protagonist who has discovered the paradox on which so-called utopian happiness is based. In this scene, the Benefactor explains to D-503 the complex nature of utopian happiness and the benevolent intentions behind it. In his revelations, the Benefactor provides an argument that is indebted to Dostoevsky's Grand Inquisitor, a figure whose shadow is present in nearly all dystopian landscapes. The argument is well known, and there is no need here to go into any great detail. It is useful to recall, however, that the Grand Inquisitor's basic premise is that people cannot be happy so long as they are free, "for nothing has ever been more insupportable for a man or a society than freedom."[14] For the Grand Inquisitor, therefore, universal happiness entails eliminating the experiences that free choice implies—the experiences of doubt, uncertainty, anxiety. He argues that people cannot be happy with bread alone; they must be provided with explicit answers to life's nagging questions, "for the secret of man's being is not to live but to have something to live for" (pp. 234–

35). But since there are no absolute truths, since the most important questions are unanswerable, people must be persuaded that they have answers even though there are none. Thus, the Inquisitor rules by deceptions—by "miracle, mystery, authority"—which provide security, comfort, and happiness for his followers, while he takes on the burden of making all decisions and resolving all ambiguities. This ensures that the people will be happy, while those who rule, like himself, heroically assume the burden of choice and are unhappy.

In *We*, the same argument is made by the Benefactor when he reveals to D-503 the principle of the perfect happiness on which the United State is founded. "Let us talk like adults," he says, "after the children have gone to bed: let us say it all, to the very end. I ask you: what did people—from their very infancy—pray for, dream about, long for? They longed for someone to tell them, once and for all, the meaning of happiness, and then to bind them to it with a chain. What are we doing now, if not this very thing? The ancient dream of paradise. . . . Remember: those in paradise no longer know desires, no longer know pity and love. There are only the blessed, with their imaginations excised . . . —angels, obedient slaves of God" (p. 214). Thus, utopian happiness, which entails the elimination of all doubt and desire, is based on a deception, a fraudulent but "noble lie"—that in utopia all uncertainties are resolved and all desires fulfilled. Like the Grand Inquisitor, the Benefactor claims to be acting out of a love for mankind, a claim that takes on tragic connotations when he compares his situation to the situation of those who took on the burden of crucifying Christ: "Does it not seem to you that the role of those above [those who nailed Christ to the cross] is the most difficult, the most important? If not for them, would this entire majestic tragedy have taken place? They were reviled by the ignorant crowd: but for that the author of the tragedy—God—should have rewarded them all the more generously" (p. 213). In *Brave New World*, the Controller observes in a similar way that "happiness is a hard master—particularly other people's happiness" (p. 154).

In revealing the deceptions, the "noble lies," on which his happy society is constructed, the Benefactor makes us aware of the complex and contradictory nature of utopian happiness. His argument achieves a complexity that the reader is unable to simply reject or endorse. The efficacy of his argument lies in its thought-provoking power. The point is not to choose either freedom or happiness, since each intersects with the other, but to become more aware of the conflicts and complex relationships between self/society, individual/community, I/we. Equally important, the Benefactor's revelations remind us that all forms of social organization—utopian or anti-utopian—are arbitrary and provisional. The potential danger of utopian values lies not in the values themselves but in the misguided effort to realize them permanently; in their full realization lies their destruction. *We* depicts this contradiction and at the same time provokes us to face a future that is open-ended—a future whose multiple possibilities and outcomes are made contingent on our own actions and decisions.

In the preface to *Last and First Men* (1930), a fictive history of the future of mankind, the utopian writer Olaf Stapledon observed that "we all desire the future to turn out more happily. . . . In particular we desire our present civilization to advance steadily toward some kind of utopia. The thought that it may decay or collapse, and that all its spiritual treasure may be lost irrevocably, is repugnant to us. Yet this must be faced as at least a possibility."[15] In Stapledon's philosophical meditations on the future, utopia is a provisional phase, a stage in the development of "waking worlds." For Stapledon, this is the happiest phase, marked by true balance between self and community, what he called "personality-in-community." This utopian ideal avoids both excessive egoism, which leads to a

118

failure to live responsibly with others, and excessive community, which can lead to a mysticism of the state or race and in which the individual is lost in "one unanimous and harmonious ant-heap" (*The Brothers Karamazov,* p. 237). Genuine community strives for a dialectical balance between the two, but this balance is a fragile one that constantly shifts, allowing slips into one extreme or the other.

It is precisely the possibility that the future can also turn out badly that anti-utopias have faced honestly and directly. The possibilities envisioned in this literature range from the brutal totalitarianism of *Nineteen Eighty-Four* and the mindless "happiness" of *We* and *Brave New World* to nuclear holocaust, overpopulation, the poisoning of the environment, takeovers by machine intelligence, technocracy, and so on, depicted in such works as Ellison's *Boy and His Dog,* Burgess's *Clockwork Orange,* Christopher's *No Blade of Grass,* Vonnegut's *Player Piano,* Brunner's *Sheep Look Up,* Lem's *Futurological Congress,* Bradbury's *Fahrenheit 451,* Dick's *Do Androids Dream of Electric Sheep?,* and many others. To the extent that these works do not attempt to legitimize the status quo or to recover some idealized image of the past, they are not one-sided efforts to discredit the whole utopian tradition. Rather, they forcibly remind us that utopia is by no means a historical inevitability; they bring the question of utopia within the horizon of history.

But this creates a sobering change. For if we admit history, contingency, and change to utopia, if we tear down the Green Wall and let the winds blow freely, then how do we distinguish utopia from the rest of society? If we admit the experiences of doubt, conflict, uncertainty, and anxiety, then have we not reached the end of utopia? What remains of utopia once we accept the inevitability of history and change? What remains, of course, is the impulse toward improvement, now perhaps more sober and more urgent than before. By demonstrating the necessity of history, the anti-utopia does not constitute the end of utopia but can become a stimulus, an opportunity to reinvigorate utopia by means of a critical revaluation of its basic premises and assumptions.

6

The Ambiguous Utopia
A Third Alternative

Utopia too must have a history.

— H. G. WELLS, *A Modern Utopia*

The critical inversions of utopian values that we find in such anti-utopias as Zamyatin's *We* and Huxley's *Brave New World* effectively bring into focus the limitations of the static or closed utopia. These inversions relentlessly expose the closed utopia where it is most vulnerable: in its desire to escape the uncertainties of time and history and in its reduction of social complexity to a single vision, a vision that strains to represent a stable and ultimate social accomplishment. In revealing the paradoxes and dangers of such single-minded undertakings, the anti-utopian critique overlooks the potential critical power of the dialectical structure of the closed utopia and directs its attack, also rather single-mindedly at times, on the timeless and perfect solutions to which the reader is asked to assent. Thus, the full force of the anti-utopian critique is directed primarily at those boundaries that enclose utopia and set it apart as an "other" place of social harmony and happiness. These boundaries, however, are now seen as signs of alienation and containment, as barriers that repress and constrain human possibilities rather than enhance them. From the utopian perspective, as we have seen, these boundaries are necessary to guarantee freedom and happiness; from the anti-utopian perspective, however, they are seen to keep the inhabitants captive, reducing their possibilities for freedom and happiness to a uniformity and conformity that threatens the very possibility of social alternatives and even of conscious life. The crucial paradox, of course, is that if utopia retains its boundaries, if it continues to exclude conflict, contradictions, and history, then it runs the risk of congealing into Zamyatin's entropic paradise, Huxley's world of mindless pleasure, or even Orwell's fascist dictatorship; and if utopia tears down its boundaries and opens its gates to history, change, and process, then it loses its very identity and becomes indistinguishable from the social reality it tries to displace.

The dilemma posed by this paradox is an important one for both writers and readers of utopian fiction. One way out of this dilemma may be to reject all utopian efforts as hopelessly contradictory and to turn to anti-utopias, as many writers of science fiction have done. Such an option is not entirely satisfactory, however, since anti-utopias are also inherently reductive, leaving us with a single menacing vision of society, a vision, moreover, which may have the unproductive effect of affirming the status quo. If we are to reject utopian narrative because it constrains us with a formulaic solution that oversimplifies social problems, then we must also reject anti-utopian narrative because it is no less formulaic in its final, often terrifying conclusions. But if we are not willing to reject either, then the question becomes how to acknowledge the powerful anti-utopian critique without sacrificing the significant benefits of the utopian impulse and utopian desire for social alternatives. If history is an infinite process, as Zamyatin's novel demonstrates so powerfully, then there can no longer be any question of social perfection, of closed systems, of fixed boundaries, of an absolute cognition of the good society. What we have instead are contingency, relativism, difference, multiplicity, plurality—a world, in other words, that is subjectively experienced by different individuals and different groups of individuals who grasp it in essentially different ways. In such a world, every utopian solution is bound to prove false: utopian harmony and happiness cannot be objectively determined, and history cannot be defined once and for all, since both are produced by a dialectical and therefore open-ended interaction among subjects and social groups whose values change as their experience changes and as time unfolds.

Utopian narrative must therefore do away with the notion of an "untroubled region" of social perfection for all and attempt to expand the utopian horizon by providing utopian societies. In this way, utopian narrative can take as its task a constant reworking of our social dreams and a permanent revising of utopian desire—all within the context of a grasp of history. Such a shift in priorities implies a rejection of the utopian craving for permanence and enclosure and a transformation of the structure of the closed utopia. It implies an "open-ended utopia," as Bülent Somay has pointed out, that "portrays a utopian locus as a mere phase in the infinite unfolding of the utopian horizon."[1] Such an ambiguous utopia would be self-consciously indeterminate and incomplete and would involve the reader in a more active way; it would, in fact, invite the reader to participate in the dialectical process by which all utopias are constructed. An "open-ended" utopia would necessarily have to take on the characteristics of Eco's "open" text, which, as we have seen, requires the reader to play a more fundamental organizing role as the constructor of the text's meaning.[2]

An example of a utopian narrative that attempts to go beyond the limitations of the closed utopia by exploring the possibilities of an open-ended or historical model is H. G. Wells's *Modern Utopia* (1905). In this work Wells observes that "the whole trend of modern thought is against the permanence of any . . . enclosures," and he proposes a "kinetic" utopia that dispenses with the traditional utopian longing for certainty and perpetual rest.[3] Such a "modern" utopia, Wells insists, must be synthetic in its overall approach: "The modern Utopia is to be, before all things, synthetic. Politically and socially, as linguistically, we must suppose it a synthesis" (p. 212). Such a synthesis, according to Wells, is more open to diversity, difference, and contingency; it embraces neither a single-minded endorsement of utopian values nor an unconditional rejection of all utopian efforts. Instead, Wells's modern utopia assumes a more detached position encompassing both utopian and anti-utopian perspectives, a position that allows him to propose utopian alternatives at the same time that he remains skeptical and doubtful, questioning his own proposals even as he makes them. This conjunction of utopian hope and anti-utopian skepticism leads Morson to identify Wells's "modern" utopia as a "meta-utopia," distinguishing it from both the closed utopia and the entropic dystopia.[4] Wells's "kinetic" model of utopia, in other words, acknowledges the importance of utopian dreams and values but rejects the facile optimism of the ahistorical utopia and the futile cynicism of the anti-utopia.

The distinguishing features of Wells's open-ended utopia are immediately evident in its narrative structure, which is designed to provide the reader with a number of contradictory and inconclusive perspectives on utopian values. This structure, as we have seen, was already apparent to some extent in More's *Utopia*, with its contentious voices and open-ended dialogue. In *A Modern Utopia*, however, this structure reaches a higher level of complexity. In Wells's text we need to distinguish among three distinct voices: the author of "A Note to the Reader," which is signed "H. G. Wells"; "the Owner of the Voice," who is the principal narrator of this modern utopia; and "the intrusive chairman," the editor of the book who writes the first and last chapters in italics.

In "A Note to the Reader," "Wells" explains that this work is not a traditional "argumentative essay" that provides the reader with two alternatives, but a "multiplex presentation" that requires the reader to go beyond the Manichean either/or arguments of the closed utopia. "Wells" notes that the classical utopia is "a form which appeals most readily to what is called the 'serious' reader, the reader who is often no more than the solemnly impatient parasite of great questions." Such a reader, "Wells" goes on to say, "likes everything in hard, heavy lines, black and white, yes and no, because he does not understand how much there is that cannot be presented at all that way; wherever there is any levity of humour or difficulty of multiplex presentation, he refuses attention. Mentally he seems built up upon an invincible assumption that the Spirit of Creation cannot count beyond two, he deals only in alternatives" (p. xxxi). Such a reader will be disappointed by *A Modern Utopia*.

In arriving at "the peculiar method" of this utopian narrative, "Wells" explains that he "spent some vacillating months over the scheme of the book." He considered first the form of "the discussion novel," but this form entailed distracting complications among the characters. Next he attempted "to cast the thing into a shape resembling Boswell's Johnson, a sort of interplay between monologue and commentary." And after rejecting "hard narrative" on the grounds that this would "pander to the vulgar appetite for dark stories," "Wells" decided on its present form, "a sort of shot-silk texture" that provides us with an account of utopian experiences that is different from previous accounts in several ways.

As the "intrusive chairman" informs us in the next section, the text of this modern utopia will be spoken by a "voice" which *"is not to be taken as the Voice of the ostensible author who fathers these pages"* (p. 1). This unauthoritative voice belongs to the traveler to utopia who admits quite candidly that his journey to utopia takes place entirely in his imagination. "We are here," he states, "by an act of the imagination and that is one of those metaphysical operations that are so difficult to make credible" (p. 133). Unlike previous travelers to utopia, who find themselves shipwrecked on a hitherto unknown island or who travel in time to an unknown future, this traveler's account of utopian experiences is merely *"the story of the adventure of his soul among Utopian inquiries"* (p. 2). Furthermore, this voice is accompanied on this imaginary journey by another "earthly person," an anti-utopian botanist who is antagonistic to "the Owner of the Voice" and who reminds him from time to time that all utopias are "fanciful, useless dreams" (p. 357).

The purpose of this venture into "utopian inquiries" will not be the formulation of a faultless image of utopian happiness, but a critical investigation of utopian values, a tentative exploration of the kinds of problems that one encounters in trying to envision a "modern" utopia. Essentially, this involves raising a number of anti-utopian objections. "The Owner of the Voice" finds, for example, that past utopias have shown an utter disregard for history and have devalued the importance of freedom and individuality. In exposing the limitations of "those finite compact settlements of the older school of dreamers" (p. 123), he is particularly critical of their absolute certainty and dogmatic prescriptiveness:

> So long as we ignore difference, so long as we ignore individuality . . . we can make absolute statements, prescribe communisms or individualisms, and all sorts of hard theoretic arrangements. But in the world of reality, which . . . is nothing more or less than the world of individuality, there are no absolute rights and wrongs, there are no qualitative questions at all, but only quantitative adjustments. (Pp. 36–37)

In identifying a number of other features that have made the closed utopia problematic, "the Owner of the Voice" singles out its "very definite artistic limitations" (p. 9) and its reductiveness: "There must always be a certain effect of hardness and thinness about Utopian speculations" (p. 9). A more fundamental shortcoming is indicated by his observation that since "most Utopias present themselves as going concerns, as happiness in being," they "make it an essential condition that a happy land can have no history" (p. 135). It is this limitation, as we have seen, that makes the closed utopia so vulnerable to anti-utopian attacks.

In uncovering these limitations, Wells's "adventure among Utopian inquiries" remains tentative, fragmentary, and inconclusive. Instead of establishing certainties and reaching final conclusions, Wells's open-ended exploration demonstrates that "a Utopia is a thing of the imagination that becomes more and more fragile with every added circumstance, that, like a soap-bubble, . . . is most brilliantly and variously coloured at the very instant of its dissolution" (p. 352). What we experience in reading this ambiguous utopia is what "the Owner of the Voice" describes as "the thrust and disturbance of . . . insurgent movement" (p. 20). For in reading this utopian narrative, as the chairman explains, we are to imagine "the Owner of the Voice" on a stage *"sitting at a table reading a manuscript about Utopias"* (p. 2). We are to imagine that behind him is a screen *"on which moving pictures intermittently appear."* The chairman emphasizes that *"the image of a cinematograph entertainment is the one to grasp"* (p. 3). He goes on to suggest that the utopian "Owner of the Voice" and the anti-utopian botanist are two principal actors, or antagonists, whose arguments and counterarguments we are to imagine as a kind of spectacle on the screen: *"There will be an effect of these two people going to and fro in front of the circle of a rather defective lantern, which sometimes jambs and sometimes gets out of focus, but which does occasionally succeed in displaying on the screen a momentary moving picture of Utopian conditions"* (pp. 3–4).

In comparing the experience of reading this utopian narrative with the experience of watching a defective film, the chairman indicates the kind of effect this presentation is intended to have on its readers. The metaphor of a moving film, with its continually changing images, reinforces the central theme of *A Modern Utopia*, which is that "there is no perfection, there is no enduring treasure" (p. 233). To counter the rigidity and timelessness of the closed utopia, this "kinetic" utopia is to be perceived as constantly moving, changing, going in and out of focus. The overall effect of this, as the chairman describes it, is one of "lucid vagueness" rather than clear definition and delineation. Unlike the closed utopia, then, which may be compared to a freeze-frame in its fixed objectivity, this modern utopia is a "moving picture" that presents itself to us from a number of different perspectives and different points of view. Similar to the process of watching a film, in which we observe a series of images which we must connect and imbue with significance, the process of reading this utopia will involve our own activity in connecting fragmentary images, filling in gaps and omissions in the narrative, and determining the significance and meaning of the whole. Like the spectators of a film, we alternate between identifying with the utopian images presented to us and distancing ourselves from them. In this dialectical interaction, the reader may experience moments of insight and lucidity and moments of skepticism and doubt. And since Wells's exploration of utopian values is open-ended, the reader is set free to go beyond the boundaries of the text to envision her own utopian alternatives. In a very real sense, then, Wells's ambiguous utopia reminds us that utopia is a no-place, an indeterminate territory that cannot be objectively defined and fixed in time and space. As "dream stuff," its location cannot be delineated on any map, real or imaginary; for Wells, utopia emerges momentarily, in the interplay between utopian desire and anti-utopian doubt, and fades again just as quickly as the images on the movie screen.

In the final chapter, entitled "The Bubble Bursts," the chairman raises a number of questions about the form and content of this work. What are we to make, he asks, of *"this irascible little man of the Voice, this impatient dreamer, this scolding Optimist, who has argued so rudely and dogmatically . . . . And . . . why was he intruded?"* (p. 371). Why, in other words, the different voices in the text and the "peculiar method" by which this utopia is presented? *"Why could not a modern Utopia be discussed without this impersonation—impersonally? It has confused the book, you say, made the argument hard to follow, and thrown a quality of insincerity over the whole. Are we but mocking at Utopias, you demand, using all these noble and generalized hopes as a backcloth against which two bickering personalities jar and squabble?"* (p. 371). It is important that, unlike the closed utopia, this utopia ends with questions rather than answers. *"There is a common notion,"* the chairman explains, *"that the reading of a Utopia should end with a swelling heart and clear resolves, with lists of names, formations of commit- tees, and even the commencement of subscriptions. But this Utopia began upon a philosophy of fragmentation, and ends, confusedly, amidst a gross tumult of immediate realities, in dust and doubt, with, at the best, one individual's aspiration. Utopias were once in good faith, projects for a fresh creation of the world and of a most unworldly completeness; this so-called Modern Utopia is a mere story of personal adventures among Utopian philosophies"* (pp. 371–72).

Self-consciously incomplete and contradictory, this ambig- uous utopia patently offers the reader not a single "un- worldly" vision of social perfection but *"two visions . . . each commenting on the other"* (pp. 371–72). Because these visions remain unreconciled and incompatible, they leave the reader suspended between utopian and anti-utopian positions. In his final statement, the chairman admits that *"in that in- congruity between great and individual inheres the incompatibility I could not resolve, and which, therefore, I have had to present in this conflicting form"* (p. 373). It is this "conflicting form" that acti- vates the reader, stimulating the desire for utopia at the same time that it emphasizes the limitations of all utopian efforts. Like Zamyatin's *We*, *A Modern Utopia* demonstrates that there are no perfect systems and no final answers, and that all efforts to erect firm spatial boundaries in a landscape of time are illusory and futile. What makes Wells's modern utopia open-ended is the recognition of the reality of history; for if, as Wells believes, "Utopia too must have a history," then it can no longer be represented as a timeless region frozen under an eternal sky—it can only be approximated through a dialectical interplay of social tensions and contradictions, or, as Wells put it, through "the experimental inconsistency of an enquiring man" (p. 209).

Wells's modifications of classical utopian narrative attempt to move beyond the limitations of the closed or ahistorical model by extending the possibilities for open-endedness. In turning to more recent examples of utopian fiction, we find that Wells's ambiguous utopia has had different levels of influence. Some utopian narratives—Marge Piercy's *Woman on the Edge of Time* (1976) and Ursula K. Le Guin's *The Dispossessed* (1974), for example—have tried to build on Wells's "multiplex presentation" in order to expand the utopian horizon of their readers. These narratives are self-consciously open in the sense that the task of constructing utopia is left incomplete in the text or is threatened in some significant way so that the cooperation and participation of the reader is required to achieve completion or closure. Other utopian narratives— Huxley's *Island* (1962), B. F. Skinner's *Walden Two* (1948), and Ernest Callenbach's *Ecotopia* (1975)—while structured like closed texts in the sense that they provide us with a single vision that claims to represent and exhaust utopian possibilities, can also be read as ambiguous utopias.[5] Like Wells's model, these narratives are much more concerned with the need for difference and diversity and with the irreducible existential experiences of suffering and death, all of which they try to integrate into the fabric of the social life they represent. Also, following Wells, these narratives can be seen to reflect, to a greater or lesser degree, the crucial impact of historical consciousness on the traditional utopian craving for completeness, security, and enclosure. Since all these narratives try to come to terms with the anti-utopian critique, they can be seen to represent what Huxley called a "third alternative"—an option that avoids both the heady confidence and the easy consolation of some closed utopias and the potentially crippling apathy of some anti-utopias. This alternative attempts to make the reader aware of both utopian and anti-utopian possibilities and enhances the reader's role in the potential realization of one or the other. In focusing directly on the reader's role, this alternative makes explicit the more active role for the reader that was implicit in the classical model of utopia.

In his 1946 foreword to *Brave New World*, Huxley speculated about this alternative when he imagined a "hypothetical new version" of his novel. "If I were to rewrite the book," he explained, "I would offer the Savage a third alternative. Between the utopian and the primitive horns of his dilemma would lie the possibility of sanity." Huxley went on to suggest that this possibility would be based on decentralized economics, cooperative politics, the selective use of science and technology to enhance life, and a religion that "would be the conscious and intelligent pursuit of man's Final End."[6] Instead of a Manichean opposition between utopian and anti-utopian extremes, in other words, Huxley here advocates a more pragmatic alternative: a dialectical synthesis of the possibilities that exist between these extremes.

To see what such a "third alternative" looks like, we need only consider Huxley's utopian novel *Island*.[7] The principles upon which this vision of utopia is constructed are those of balance and integration. Huxley's approach, like Wells's, is synthetic: essentially, Huxley attempts to balance Eastern religious values and Western science and technology. The result is that the inhabitants of his imaginary island of Pala are both happy and free: they have successfully blended Buddhism and experimental science, psychedelic drugs and behavioral

131

engineering, pastoral values and technology. On Pala, this synthesis has produced a rich and rewarding life in which everyone lives in harmony with nature and spends a great deal of time cultivating an authentic relationship to his mortality. To intensify their existential awareness of time and death, the Palanese have taught the many mynah birds on the island to repeat incessantly the words "attention" and "here and now."

What casts a dark dystopian shadow over Huxley's happy island is not its techniques of behavioral engineering nor its obsession with mortality, but the "brave new world" that surrounds it on all sides. Disregarding Wells's caution against "finite compact settlements," Huxley isolates his utopian community—"a community of exiles and refugees from the Brave New World"—behind fragile boundaries.[8] Insulated on one side by a "semi-circle of mountains" and on the other by "miles of rock-bound coast" (p. 20), Pala has gone unnoticed by the rest of society. These boundaries have served to conceal it over the years, protecting it against the greed, exploitation, and world wars that have taken place outside its borders. When oil is discovered nearby, however, Pala's boundaries are no significant obstacle to "the great world of impersonal forces and proliferating numbers, . . . collective paranoias [and] organized diabolism" (p. 294). Pala simply doesn't have "a ghost of a chance" when it comes to oil cartels, quick profits, and the Sears and Roebuck spring and summer catalog. Powerless and defenseless, this island surrounded by "walls" is quickly engulfed by the implacable march of history, leaving no trace of its former existence. As in Zamyatin's *We*, the walls once again come down. This time, however, there is no "green wind" of liberation blowing from end to end; there is only the force of history, a very dystopian history, which no utopian boundaries can withstand. It's as if Pala were a demonstration of the veracity of Wells's observation in *A Modern Utopia*: "We are acutely aware nowadays that, however subtly contrived [a utopia] may be, outside [its] boundary lines the epidemic, the breeding barbarian or the economic power, will gather its strength to overcome [it]. The swift march of invention is all for the invader" (pp. 11–12).

Because Pala perishes so decisively, it argues for the hopelessness of constructing utopias outside of history or behind fixed barriers. But the efficacy of Huxley's "third alternative" remains intact. For in exposing the limits of the enclosed utopia, Huxley also demonstrates the need for an open-ended utopia based on a dialectical awareness of the possibilities that exist "here and now." For Huxley, this entails a selective synthesis of the possibilities available to us; and because these possibilities are constantly changing, so is any potential synthesis. Huxley's ambiguous utopia, in other words, is not a stable and ultimate place (it is, more accurately, a no-place at the end of the novel), but a state of mind—an awareness of social possibilities that exist between the utopian and the anti-utopian "horns of the dilemma" and a readiness to confront the contradictions of this dilemma in the absence of the secure boundaries that the enclosed utopia provides.

Other closed utopian narratives are less willing to confront these contradictions and are therefore less productive in extending the reader's utopian horizon. Skinner's *Walden Two*, for example, provides us with a complete blueprint for utopian happiness. In this respect Skinner's model is a regression to the "finite compact settlements of the older school of dreamers" that Wells rejected. What distinguishes Skinner's utopian vision is his readiness to defend the closed utopia and his willingness to provide it with a tool, the science of human engineering, that makes it in effect the most thoroughly conditioned of utopias, one in which everyone is subject to total manipulation and control.

Although Skinner seems to be aware of the limitations of the static utopia, he provides us with a model of a rigid utopia that systematically removes all ambiguity and any possibility for change. Frazier, our guide and the founder of this imaginary community, insists that Walden Two has "an active drive for the future" and that "people in Walden Two never stop changing."[9] But there is little evidence of this in the totally determined system that he describes. In fact, the experimental method that Frazier cites to assure us of the open-endedness of his community only produces more efficiency and more control in refining the principles of positive reinforcement upon which Walden Two is based. Perhaps even more disturbing is the fact that in Walden Two the study of history is expressly outlawed, as it is in most dystopias. The reason for this prohibition, we must assume, is that the study of history would make the inhabitants of Walden Two aware of the finite basis of their present social order and of the possibility of social transformation. By eliminating historical consciousness and by reducing his utopian vision to a delineation of social control, Skinner also reduces the utopian horizon of his readers. It is not surprising, then, that even though Skinner intended his utopia to be a positive vision of the good society, its effect on most readers is just the opposite: readers find very little that distinguishes *Walden Two* from such anti-utopias as *Brave New World*, *Nineteen Eighty-Four*, and Dostoevsky's "The Legend of the Grand Inquisitor."[10] Certainly Skinner's utopian vision agitates, arouses, and provokes its readers in a way that very few utopian works have, but this is not the kind of startling and unsettling effect that can make the act of reading literary utopias a productive and challenging experience; rather, for most readers, the effect of *Walden Two* is to confirm the attitudes they already hold and, indeed, to inspire them to defend these attitudes more vigorously.[11]

A similar constraining effect on the reader is produced by Ernest Callenbach's *Ecotopia*. Although not as intent as Skinner on subjecting everything and everyone to total control and domination, Callenbach offers a vision of a "stable-state" utopia that does not soar very far beyond what is already known. Based on the ecological imperative that "humans were meant to take their modest place in a seamless, stable-state web of living organisms, disturbing that web as little as possible," Callenbach provides us with a model of a closed and isolated utopian community whose ideal is harmony with the natural world.[12] Like Huxley's Pala, Ecotopia is founded on a selective synthesis of technological and pastoral values, and much about life in Ecotopia is appealing: there are various outlets for emotional and aesthetic expression and the opportunity for healthy disagreement (there is, in fact, a great deal of contentious quarreling). The biological model on which Ecotopia is constructed emphasizes "growing with" rather than competing with nature, a comparison suggesting that Ecotopia is an open-ended utopia capable of change. As one of the Ecotopians explains: "Our system meanders on its peaceful way, while yours has constant convulsions. I think of ours like a meadow in the sun. There is a lot of change going on—plants growing, other plants dying, bacteria decomposing them, mice eating seeds, hawks eating mice, a tree or two beginning to grow up and shade grasses. But the meadow sustains itself on a steady-state basis—unless men come along and mess it up" (pp. 39–40).

But ultimately, the goal of Ecotopia is equilibrium and balance. Disregarding the fate of Huxley's Pala, Callenbach locates his utopian community of exiles behind closed borders. The traditional utopian urge for separation and exclusion is not questioned in Callenbach's narrative and is, in fact, confirmed by the narrator-visitor's easy conversion to Ecotopian values. In deciding to remain within the boundaries of Ecotopia, Callenbach's narrator shows no signs of the deep-seated doubts and apprehensions that plague Skinner's narrator before he decides to remain in utopia.

Both *Walden Two* and *Ecotopia* may be read as ambiguous utopias in the sense that they make the reader aware of the problems and deficiencies of the closed utopia and try to incorporate change. But neither does this in a satisfactory way. For in presenting the reader with a single vision of the good society, a vision that claims to have resolved social discrepancies, these works are constraining in their effects. Rather than stimulating us with unresolved questions, they attempt to formulate solutions; rather than developing the possibilities of Wells's open-ended narrative, they return to the closed models of Bellamy and Cabet. For a fuller realization of Huxley's third alternative and of the possibilities inherent in Wells's "multiplex" narrative strategy, we must turn to the ambiguous utopias of Piercy and Le Guin. These open utopias attempt to expand the reader's utopian horizons by developing the complexities of a third alternative and by emphasizing the reader's role in the construction of a synthesis of utopian and anti-utopian alternatives.

Piercy's *Woman on the Edge of Time* differs from *Walden Two* and *Ecotopia* primarily in its more complex and demanding narrative structure. Piercy's novel provides us with two interrelated plots that subtly interweave powerful social criticism and imaginative utopian fantasy; it envisions not one but two possible social alternatives; and it focuses on the reader's role in determining which of these alternatives might eventually come about.

As social criticism, *Woman on the Edge of Time* is a devastating indictment of an extremely oppressive society dominated by power relations, exploitation, manipulation, and victimization. Consuelo Ramos, the heroine of the novel, is an impoverished Chicano woman, who, after a series of unfortunate and tragic events, is committed to a mental hospital where she is misdiagnosed as a chronic alcoholic and child abuser. The violence and injustices of a system of economic exploitation and social degradation that have brought her to this point are portrayed vividly in naturalistic detail: the misery and loneliness of poverty, the humiliations of a social system dominated by racial and sexual prejudices, the indifference that grinds people into total submission. Piercy's unrelenting exposition of this system of domination and indifference distinguishes her narrative from other utopias in which this kind of social analysis is presented in a more detached and diffident manner. Consuelo's victimization by this system reaches the ultimate dystopian moment when she is subjected to an experiment that involves implanting a neuro-electronic device in her brain. This operation, similar to the one in Zamyatin's *We*, is intended to control her "deviant" behavior so that she will be able to "adjust" to society; but this operation is also shown to have significant implications for the two opposing future worlds that Consuelo visits.

During her confinement in the hospital, Consuelo becomes more and more estranged from her immediate environment as she becomes increasingly familiar with a utopian one, 150 years in the future. Because of her exceptional receptiveness as a "catcher," she is able to make contact with Luciente, a representative from a future anarchist-communitarian society who becomes her guide to the utopian alternative of Mattapoisett. This utopian vision, founded on principles similar to those of Huxley's Pala, is based on economic and political decentralization, sexual and racial liberation, freedom from all forms of external domination and power, an effort to integrate science and nature, and tolerance for individual and cultural differences. Furthermore, all relations based on property have been done away with in Mattapoisett; people are generous, caring, and loving, and men and women share equally in all things, including the "mothering" of children.

Soon after her operation, however, Consuelo discovers that Mattapoisett represents only one future possibility, for there exists alongside it an anti-utopian possibility that threatens to destroy it. This other, more chilling, vision of the future extends the kind of objectification, domination, and manipulation that Consuelo has experienced in her own time. In this other version, the population consists mainly of androids, robots, and cybernauts, and the few remaining people are totally controlled and monitored by what remains of a ruling class of capitalists. In this future we find people "contracted" to each other as objects, an endless array of drugs used to escape the ugliness of the poisoned environment, women who have been biologically engineered to be sexual diversions, and the gradual disappearance of the distinctions between organic and artificial life forms. When Consuelo realizes that the success or failure of the experiments she is participating in will play an important role in determining which of these two possible futures becomes real, she takes action by poisoning the doctors and psychiatrists who are conducting the experiments. Her radical action represents her choice of the utopian future.

What makes Piercy's narrative open-ended is the dialectical conception of history underlying it. Unlike *Walden Two*, in which Frazier claims that "the past and the future are both irrelevant" (p. 174), Piercy's vision of two opposing futures is based on a conception of history in which the present, past, and future are shown to be inextricably interrelated: our choice of the future depends on our past and on what we do in the present. In Piercy's view, the future is open to variation, but the future that will take place will grow out of our present situation with its historically determined horizons and our actions within that situation. Piercy's narrative demonstrates that the individual has the capacity to choose future alternatives, and that history is therefore to a certain extent an open project; these alternatives, however, emerge from a present actuality as a consequence of the choices we make here and now. Thus, Piercy constructs her utopia on a multi-dimensional view of time in which the future is not some inevitable timetable, but is contingent on innumerable choices and actions in the absence of any certainty as to which future will come to be. For even Consuelo's radical act does not secure the realization of the utopian possibility; rather, as part of the open-ended historical process, this possibility will require an endless series of choices, a constant negation of the negation, a continual remodeling of the utopian dream.

The open-endedness of Piercy's utopian vision is made apparent toward the end of the narrative when Consuelo asks Luciente whether the struggle between Mattapoisett and its anti-utopian enemies will ever end. Luciente replies: "How is it ever over? . . . In time the sun goes nova. Big bang. What else? We renew, we regenerate. Or die."[13] Luciente then describes her own utopian dream, indicating that such dreams will continue to exist even in what from our point of view appears to be utopia: "Someday," she explains, "the gross repair will be done. The oceans will be balanced, the rivers flow clean, the wetlands and the forests flourish. There'll be no more enemies. No Them and Us. We can quarrel joyously with each other about important matters of idea and art. The vestiges of old ways will fade. I can't know that time—anymore than you can ultimately know us. We can only know what we can truly imagine" (p. 328). Utopia, in other words, cannot be known objectively and fixed in a timeless and brilliant landscape; it can only be desired and struggled for against a constantly changing historical horizon, a horizon that opens to diverse possibilities.

Woman on the Edge of Time, then, challenges the reader, not with a stable-state vision of utopia, but with a precariously open vision that acknowledges both utopian and anti-utopian possibilities. In making the reader aware of his or her own role in shaping the future that will be, Piercy shows that the struggle for utopia depends on our actions in an open-ended historical process.

Another ambiguous utopia that examines the tensions and conflicts between utopian and anti-utopian possibilities without providing the satisfaction of a conclusive utopian solution is Ursula Le Guin's *The Dispossessed*. Originally subtitled *An*

Ambiguous Utopia, this work projects two fictive worlds in the form of two parallel planets, each of which contains utopian and anti-utopian potentials and neither of which is purely a good-place or a bad-place.[14] In focusing on the social, political, and ethical differences that distinguish these two worlds, Le Guin shifts her narrative perspective and interests. Instead of providing us with concrete representations of either a utopian or an anti-utopian alternative, as Piercy does, Le Guin leaves this task up to the reader. And unlike Piercy's narrative, in which the threat to utopia comes from the outside, Le Guin's narrative locates this threat inside the boundaries of utopia itself. The effect of these changes is to suspend the reader between a number of unresolved oppositions and multiple points of view. Since Le Guin's text, in other words, focuses on the plurality and multiplicity of utopian and anti-utopian possibilities, the burden of producing a selective synthesis or an image of utopia proper is shifted entirely to the reader. This makes the reader an active partner in the dialectical process of utopian construction, enfolding her in the very activity of producing a possible utopian representation. In reading *The Dispossessed,* then, the reader is aware of the indeterminacy of utopia in the sense that as a genuine no-place in space and time, it is also "no-place" in the text itself; it emerges instead in the dialectical interplay of the numerous contradictions that the text takes up. The essential recognitions that inform this open-ended narrative structure are that no single vision of utopian social arrangements can resolve all problems, mediate all oppositions, or reconcile all differences; and that the modern utopia, as Wells pointed out, must allow for diversity, difference, and a plurality of utopian possibilities.

With this aim in view, it is fitting that Le Guin begins her equivocal exploration of utopian and anti-utopian possibilities by calling attention to those problematic barriers that identify the closed utopia:

There was a wall. It did not look important. It was built of uncut rocks roughly mortared. An adult could look right over it, and even a child could climb it. Where it crossed the roadway, instead of having a gate it degenerated into mere geometry, a line, an idea of a boundary. But the idea was real. It was important. For seven generations there had been nothing more important than that wall.

Like all walls it was ambiguous, two-faced. What was inside it and what was outside depended upon which side of it you were on. (P. 1)

As in Zamyatin's *We*, the ambiguity of all boundaries is the central theme of Le Guin's novel. In setting alternating chapters of her narrative on opposing planets—one more or less utopian, the other more or less dystopian—Le Guin provides us with inside and outside perspectives on each. And since each planet is identified by numerous "walls," the reader is unable simply to endorse or reject either; rather, the reader is encouraged to envision that third alternative which, in the context of the novel, would be a world without walls. This alternative is neither strictly utopian nor strictly anti-utopian, but, as in Zamyatin's novel, it is "anti-entropic" and thoroughly historical.

In Le Guin's narrative, the "walls" that separate the ambiguous worlds of Anarres and Urras are represented by the miles of space between them. These binary worlds share a common history, science, and cultural tradition, but their social, economic, and political organization and their ethical values are different and distinct. Anarres, the "utopian" alternative, is inhabited by a group of anarchists and dissidents who have established a cooperative society on a bleak and barren planet. By eliminating the need for possessions and competition, they have also eliminated the need for domination, exploitation, aggression. They are a community of "dispossessed" in the sense that they have no property rela-

141

tionships with things, ideas, or people, and hence social and interpersonal relations on Anarres are free from outside determination. But unlike Mattapoisett and Pala, which offer their inhabitants a landscape of abundance, natural variety, and sensual pleasure, Anarres offers a landscape that is harsh and arid and a climate that is extremely hostile and life-denying. On this cruel planet there is no natural variety, no animal life, few sensual delights, only scarcity. Le Guin's inversion of the expected pleasant utopian setting into an extremely unpleasant one produces an ambiguous utopia indeed, one whose very existence and survival are made to depend on the collective and cooperative struggle of the community against the hardships of a brutal environment.

Urras, by contrast, is a beautiful, fertile, and prosperous planet, rich in natural resources and diverse life forms. A transparent fictionalization of Earth, Urras is a vital and luxurious place, teeming with contradictions and possibilities. As the "anti-utopian" alternative, however, it is also possessed by possessions. Representing an ultimate consumer society, Urras is a place in which everything is packaged and sold as a commodity. Since life on Urras is intensely competitive, there is widespread exploitation, manipulation, and poverty. Social and political relations are based on power and dominance—which take the form of wars between nation-states—class and sexual discrimination, and power politics. The antagonistic nations that make up this planet are easily recognizable: A-Io corresponds to the United States, a rich capitalist state with massive shopping centers and an abundance of consumer goods; and Thu, the equivalent of the Soviet Union, is a highly centralized state with a repressive form of socialism. There is also an impoverished Third World which the two superpowers exploit and dominate.

By juxtaposing two such imperfect worlds, Le Guin removes the possibility of one simply cancelling out the other and forces a situation in which each illuminates the other's strengths and deficiencies. To illustrate the limitations of each, Le Guin portrays both planets as constrained by a number of "walls." On Anarres, these "walls" become apparent in the attempt to deny history and in the paranoiac desire for separation and exclusion. To secure their "utopian" way of life, the Anarresti are convinced that only a complete rupture with their dystopian past can guarantee their future. In the effort to escape their history, they construct boundaries against the outside world, and in the process their community becomes a closed and "arrested" society. Shevek, the hero of the novel, gradually recognizes his society's repressiveness when he tries to publish his scientific theories and encounters a rigid bureaucracy that censors and appropriates his findings. Soon other constraining "walls" become apparent to him: the pressure to conform, various forms of domination, the suppression of dissent, subtle forms of manipulation. Realizing that these developments are contradictory to the values of a free "utopian" society, Shevek decides on his mission to break down the "walls" that threaten it: "I'm going to unbuild walls" (p. 267). In trying to expand the utopian horizon of his community, Shevek returns to the mother planet and to the past. His return, however, is not a rejection of the principles of his society; rather, he returns in order to rediscover the initial utopian impulse upon which Anarres was founded. Contrary to the usual pattern, in which a visitor from anti-utopia travels to utopia, Shevek leaves his dissatisfactory utopia to return to his dystopian origins. By inverting this pattern, Le Guin suggests that utopia may, at times, entail a going backward in history, if the effort is to recover the essential utopian impulse for renewal and regeneration.

What Shevek finds upon his arrival on Urras is, of course, more "walls." For if his own society has constructed various boundaries against its historical past, Urras has constructed boundaries against its future and its almost limitless possibilities. In trying to maintain the status quo, Urras has squandered its resources and wealth in maintaining large armies and police forces that brutally suppress those who attempt to change the existing system. But Shevek also finds Urras more promising than his barren homeland because it is rich in contrasts and contradictions: there is racial and economic exploitation, but there is also intellectual brilliance and cultural diversity; there is alienation and fragmentation, but there is also the possibility for rebellion; there is apathy and cynicism, but there is also exuberance and vitality. Shevek's unique perspective as a visitor from utopia on a journey through dystopia redirects our attention to the source of both utopian and anti-utopian possibilities—the contradictions and disparities that inspire utopian dreams and fuel utopian desires in the first place.

In this way, Le Guin exposes the anti-utopian limitations of utopia and the utopian possibilities in anti-utopia. These dialectical inversions put the reader in touch with the constraints and contradictions inherent in each and with the inescapable contradictions that are part of any effort to envision utopia. What is not represented in Le Guin's narrative is that third alternative, a place without walls, a selective synthesis that would reconcile these disparate worlds. Such a synthesis implies a fixed image, an enclosed world set off by determinate boundaries. Le Guin leaves the task of constructing such a potential synthesis up to the reader. For a utopia without boundaries must be based on a dialectical conception of history and cannot be defined once and for all; it can only be pursued as an elusive hope that constantly exceeds our historical horizons. As Shevek recognizes toward the end of the novel:

> Things change, change. You cannot have anything. . . .
> And least of all can you have the present, unless you
> accept with it the past and the future. Not only the past
> but also the future, not only the future but also the past!

Because they are real: only their reality makes the present real. (Pp. 280–81)

If change is "the essential function of life" (p. 267), as Shevek discovers in his journey, then no single form of social organization can ever be complete or final, and utopia too must be constantly remodeled and rethought. This makes the utopian desire for permanence and rest a paradoxical desire, a desire to construct regions of perfection in a landscape of time and change. Le Guin indicates the paradox of this desire in Shevek's "Temporal Theory," which attempts to reconcile sequential time and simultaneity. In its desire to balance change and permanence, this theory serves to underscore the contradictions at the heart of all utopian efforts. To integrate change and permanence is an ideal that exceeds our conceptual and imaginative grasp, and yet it is "the road of paradoxes," as Zamyatin put it in *We*, that is "the only road worthy of a fearless mind" (p. 117). To give up the utopian dream of a perfect and timeless paradise is not to give up the paradoxical and more elusive utopian hope, a hope that will make itself known as long as there are contradictions, a hope that will manifest itself in the gap between our utopian desires and our constantly changing historical reality.

In refusing to provide the reader with a clear delineation of utopian perfection, Le Guin leaves him with a number of unresolved questions: What are the utopian possibilities within capitalism, socialism, anarchism? Is a utopian society possible within a consumer society? Is human solidarity possible only when conditions of extreme scarcity make it necessary for survival? Do abundance, variety, and diversity inevitably lead to exploitation, discrimination, victimization? On what basis can the conflicts between utopia and anti-utopia be resolved? These questions are clearly intended to provoke the reader and stimulate his own utopian desires, recognizing that utopia will always be provisional and subject to its own contradictions.

Thus, the open-ended utopias of Piercy and Le Guin signifi-
cantly transform the narrative structure of the closed utopia.
They reject the ahistorical model located in a homogeneous
region along with its consoling vision of perfect social relations
and replace it with one that is dialectically open and historical.
The effect of this transformation, however, is not to blot out the
utopian horizon, but to extend it by awakening in the reader
that initial utopian impulse for change and rejuvenation that,
as Shevek discovers, entails a continual breaking down of the
walls that isolate us and alienate us from our own possibilities.
It is an impulse that is only implicit in the narrative strategies of
the closed utopia but is made explicit in the narrative strategies
of Piercy and Le Guin.

This more active role for the implied reader is, I think, the
most important innovation of the ambiguous utopia. Le Guin
dedicated *The Dispossessed* "for the partner," which can be read,
I think, as a reference to the reader and the kind of open-
ended, ongoing dialogue that her narrative inspires. Elsewhere Le Guin has described the act of reading as just such a
partnership in which the reader is an active participant rather
than a passive consumer:

> As you read [a book] word by word and page by page, you
> participate in its creation, just as a cellist playing a Bach
> suite participates, note by note, in the creation, the com-
> ing-to-be, the existence, of the music. And, as you read
> and re-read, the book of course participates in the creation
> of you, your thoughts and feelings, the size and temper of
> your soul. Where, in all this, does the author come in?
> Like the God of the eighteenth century deists, before you
> and the book met each other. The author's work is done,
> complete; the ongoing work, the present act of creation, is
> the collaboration by the words that stand on the page and
> the eyes that read them.[15]

As a partner in the "act of creation," the reader must be given
some task to perform, some unfinished project to complete. In

The Dispossessed, this essential task is the production of utopia itself, that paradoxical third alternative that exists somewhere between the contradictory and heterogeneous worlds that Le Guin describes. By shifting this task to the reader, Le Guin challenges us to test our own conceptual and imaginative powers within the open-ended structure of her experimental novel.

The fundamental purpose of Le Guin's narrative strategy, then, is to engage the reader in a process of interrogation and experimentation. Le Guin herself has described her approach to writing in terms of such a "thought-experiment," the function of which is to entertain alternatives and variations:

> Physicists often do thought-experiments. Einstein shoots a light-ray through a moving elevator; Schrödinger puts a cat in a box. There is no elevator, no cat, no box. The experiment is performed, the question is asked, in the mind. Einstein's elevator, Schrödinger's cat . . . are simply a way of thinking. They are questions, not answers; process, not stasis. One of the essential functions of science fiction, I think, is precisely this kind of question-asking: reversals of an habitual way of thinking, metaphors for what our language has no words for as yet, experiments in the imagination.[16]

As an inconclusive "experiment in the imagination," *The Dispossessed* explores variations and alternatives in order to expand the limited perspective of the finite or closed utopia. The aim of such an experiment is neither to predict some ultimate future nor to describe it in detail, but to sharpen our perception of possibilities, to give us critical access to the possibilities for variation that exist here and now. For even though Le Guin does not provide us with a concrete representation of a utopian alternative, she does indicate what such an alternative would entail. This alternative is implied in Shevek's "Temporal Theory," which makes instantaneous communication between diverse cultures and distant worlds possible. Shevek's theory can be read as a metaphor for utopian potentiality itself: the

147

possibility of "unbuilding the walls" that separate and isolate people and nations, the possibility of overcoming alienation and fear of otherness. In extending the possibilities inherent in Shevek's discovery, the reader is able to envision her own utopian alternative, an alternative that would involve a minimizing of the forces of exploitation and manipulation that presently determine human relationships, thus setting people free to realize other potentialities. Such variations, however, can never be thought of as final answers, but rather as part of an ongoing process of structuring and restructuring in an infinite expansion of our utopian horizons. The efficacy of Le Guin's thought-experiment lies in this cognitive function: in its capacity to stimulate us to conduct our own thought-experiments, based on the constraints that determine our social and political life and the variations that a negation of these constraints makes possible. For the real interest of such a thought-experiment, as Le Guin has stated, "is not to predict the future . . . but to describe reality, the present world."[17]

Given the enormous complexity, heterogeneity, and sheer multiplicity of our "present world," any thought-experiment of this kind is bound to be somewhat reductive. Fredric Jameson has identified the principal technique in Le Guin's utopian narratives as "world reduction," which he defines as a procedure "based on a principle of systematic exclusions, a kind of surgical excision of empirical reality, something like a process of ontological attenuation in which the sheer teeming multiplicity of what exists, of what we call reality, is deliberately thinned and weeded out through an operation of radical abstraction and simplification."[18] Such a procedure is certainly evident in *The Dispossessed* and is indeed inherent in the totalizing tendency of all utopian narrative. Le Guin's thought-experiment reduces and simplifies economic, political, and social complexities: the economic relations on Anarres are barely sketched in, political structures are vague, social relations are based on the supposition of a homogeneous population with a

148

common language and shared values in science, ethics, aesthetics, and politics. Jameson points out that on Anarres even the diversity of nature and its various life forms are systematically excluded. But the most significant exclusion in Le Guin's narrative is, of course, the representation of utopia itself, that finite image of the no-place as a determinate and ultimate place of happiness and timeless perfection.

But these reductions and exclusions, as Jameson suggests, should not be interpreted as "ideological handicaps" and attributed to the "conceptual impotence" of Le Guin's text. Nor should Le Guin's strategy of "reinforcing contradictions" be seen as an effort "to pervert any possibility for utopia," as Nadia Khouri has argued.[19] Rather, Le Guin's modification of the structure of the closed utopia can be understood, more appropriately I think, as an effort to engage the reader as a more active participant in the production of utopian values. The essential gaps and omissions in Le Guin's narrative, indeed the absence of a utopian synthesis, are part of an overall strategy to involve the reader in the very dialectical process of utopian production. As an inconclusive thought-experiment, the ambiguous utopia cannot be objectively defined, surrounded by walls, and presented as a static achievement; rather, as a place without determination—a place without walls or a place of historical potentiality—it must be constantly rethought and reworked. It would take someone with enormous speculative powers, not to mention ideological arrogance, to attempt to describe in detail a utopia in which we would all agree to live. In the meantime, the function of the ambiguous utopia is to reinforce our sense of the contradictions *and* the possibilities that define our historical situation. This twofold objective constitutes the critical value of the ambiguous utopia: to change our attitudes toward social reality and to expand our social horizons; to make us aware of the historicity of our social arrangements and to inspire us with the determination that they can be changed for the better.

7

Conclusion
The Efficacy of Contradictions

*It is certainly the fate of all Utopias
to be more or less misread.*

— H. G. WELLS, *A Modern Utopia*

This study of the activity of
reading literary utopias has sought to demonstrate how readers play an active and decisive role in determining the significance and value of utopian literature. By shifting our focus
from an exclusive concern with form and content to a more
comprehensive view of the reciprocal interaction between
readers and texts, we are able to observe how readers invest
utopias with different functions and how they infer their
meanings in different ways. To put it simply, literary utopias
mean different things to different readers because there is no
timeless essence in these (or in any) texts that reveals itself in
the same way to each reader, and because the concept of utopia is itself so multifaceted (and utopian texts are so diverse)
that any kind of consensus seems impossible. One reader's
utopia turns out, inevitably, to be another reader's nightmare.
Since all readers impose their own interests on utopias and
read these texts within their own frameworks of value, I think
it is appropriate to conclude by reiterating the principal ways
of reading utopias described here and by indicating what I

150

consider the most productive way of deriving their significance.

For the great majority of readers, utopias are understood as straightforward blueprints that map out, in great detail, rational and pragmatic alternatives to existing forms of social organization. These readers tend to evaluate utopias—both fictional and nonfictional—on the basis of their content and overt messages. They may find this content to be naive, abstract, reductive, stereotyped, and possibly even pernicious in its effects, or they may find that it constitutes a profound and inspiring model for peace and social happiness. In either case, utopias are grasped as unambiguous representations of, if not ideal, then better social relations than those existing in the author's society. Utopias, for these readers, are clearly intended for realization and implementation.

Other readers have stressed the symbolic function of these representations, arguing that utopias are not so much concrete proposals for enactment as they are projections of an imaginary time or place in which social conflicts and contradictions are only playfully resolved, cancelled, neutralized, or otherwise transformed. For these readers, the meaning of a utopian text cannot be limited to the content of its messages but must also take into account the effects these messages have on readers. Generally, these readers attempt to gauge the impact of utopias by focusing on their efficacy as symbols. Seen this way, utopias are more like thought-provoking catalysts—evocative, resonant, stimulating—than calls to action or programs for social change. This second group of readers may be further divided into two subgroups: those who understand utopias as "speculative myths" which function to mediate cultural tensions and contradictions into a more harmonious image of social life—essentially a reconciliation that balances social dissatisfactions; and those readers who see this function in terms of "an ideological critique of the domi-

151

nant ideology,"[1] a critical defamiliarization of existing social tensions that uncovers "traces" of a potentially different future manifest in the present world—an intensification of social dissatisfactions that achieves a cognitive effect.

What determines each of these approaches is, of course, the relationship that each establishes between the utopian dream of social harmony and the historical reality this dream seeks to displace. Literary utopias, as we have seen, typically map out two incongruous pictures of social life and draw attention to the disparities and discrepancies between them. It is this dialectical structuring that makes utopias such reader-oriented works. Created in opposition to existing social and political arrangements, utopias displace the old with the new— displace history with utopian fantasy—exposing the former as a region of unrealized and repressed possibilities and presenting the latter as a region of "realized" social harmony and happiness. If, as readers, we link these two regions directly, that is, if we see the former as an exposition of problems and the latter as a formulation of their solutions, then our interest will most likely be in the appropriateness, feasibility, and practicality of those solutions. If, on the other hand, we see these two regions as incongruous, inconsistent, or as Wells put it, "incommensurate," then the utopian solution is not so much a conclusive answer that cancels out, one by one, the tensions and disparities within the author's society, as it is a symbolic or, as Marin suggests, a "figurative" displacement of these tensions into an imaginary realm where they may be read as either mediated and reconciled or as estranged and dialectically intensified. Those readers who read utopias as symbolic mediations of social conflicts tend to emphasize their therapeutic effects, their consoling power as models of social harmony and cooperation; those readers who read them as dialectical intensifications of social conflicts locate their critical force in their cognitive effect, in their capacity to make social contradictions more apparent and more accessible to critical understanding.

In distinguishing these three approaches more carefully, we find that readers whose interest in utopias is restricted to the content of their visions are generally those "serious" readers, as Wells referred to them, for whom utopias are primarily designs for social action. These readers usually begin by setting utopias apart from more capricious fantasies and pure "wish-dreams" expressed in fairy tales, folktales, and other forms in which physical laws and natural processes are suspended. Insisting that utopias try to envision what is feasible in a given society, these readers often dismiss the distinction between fictional and nonfictional accounts as mere formal packaging of the serious intent. For these readers, the efficacy of utopias lies in their desirability as social alternatives, in their innovativeness, and in their pragmatic impact on political movements that seek change.

I do not want to minimize the role that utopias may have played historically in achieving important social and political reforms. Nor do I wish to suggest that utopias are unimportant for political theory and practice, for they have obviously served as models for both. Utopianism, as we have seen, encompasses a variety of forms and reflects a variety of interests and intentions. Some utopian thinkers—Owen, Fourier, Saint-Simon—constructed utopian alternatives which they felt were immediately realizable, while others—Plato, More, Morris—seem to have been less concerned with the problems of implementing their visions. Even so, in spite of the diverse intentions that may have existed among utopian authors, most readers have come to expect that utopian proposals should be concrete and feasible. "Progress," wrote Oscar Wilde, "is the realisation of utopias,"[2] and indeed, for many readers, utopias are an indispensable precondition for purposeful social change. These readers argue that utopian vi-

153

sions precede social change in the same way that thought precedes action, and they point out that many of the things we take for granted today—the eight-hour workday, social security, city planning, and any number of social programs— were all utopian dreams before they were realized, however imperfectly, in their present forms.[3] Utopias are therefore seen by these readers as models for social justice that can promote social reform. Further, these readers often cite various experiments in communal living that were based, directly or indirectly, on principles and doctrines first propounded in utopian works. These experiments, with varying degrees of success, indicate that utopian visions can have a practical impact, that utopian ideals can indeed be implemented.[4]

One might argue that all utopian designs, no matter how fantastic they may seem, are potentially realizable if there are no insurmountable physical problems and if there is sufficient practical support for them. But the efficacy of utopias does not lie solely, or even primarily, in their potential for realization. Another kind of progress is achieved in the very recognition that existing social forms can be changed and that we, the readers of utopias, can influence and shape the direction of that change. To be useful, utopias do not have to be realizable; they do not have to result in concrete action at all. Few utopian schemes have ever been implemented, even partially, and none has ever been fully realized. And the history of these efforts at realization suggests that utopias are usually deformed in the process of implementation. The inescapable paradox, as we have observed on several occasions, is that a utopia ceases to be a utopia once it is realized. As Marin, among others, has pointed out, the realization of a utopia would mean its inevitable destruction, since in the process of being realized it would lose its defining characteristic as an indeterminate no-place. Thus, utopias may be more effective if they remain within the realm of the possible. For it is precisely its status as a no-place or no-time that makes utopia so provocative. As a potential "other" to what exists, utopia is synonymous with the recurring desire to go beyond what is known, a continuing effort to transcend the forces that constrain our possibilities. The effectiveness of utopia might better be measured, then, by its capacity to change our disposition, to heighten our social expectations, to expand our social horizons, and to prepare us for action rather than by concrete results. As an unrealized possibility, utopia remains in constant opposition to existing society, an examination of the conditions of possibility that serves the essential function of making us aware of the distance that separates actuality and potentiality. By making us more conscious of the gap between what is and what might be, utopia performs the important task of increasing our awareness of the historicity of all social life and the tentativeness of all established systems of order.

Indeed, reading utopias as documents that delineate proposals for social reform may actually limit their impact on readers. For one thing, this approach reduces utopias to a mundane prescriptiveness; for another, it reduces the reader's response to either accepting or rejecting the utopian proposals provided by the text. If we choose to read utopias this way, then the only questions that need to be answered are whether the utopian proposals are practical, progressive, beneficial to all, and humane in their method of implementation.

What is evidently disregarded by this approach is the fact that the region of happiness envisioned in the text is only imaginary, and its social harmony is only just conceivable even if the utopian realm is presented as actual and "real." As a figurative construct, utopia is always located outside the boundaries of the phenomenal world; it is pure "dream stuff," as Wells observed, or a map, not of a territory, but of a "no-territory," as Marin points out.[5] Readers who emphasize the fictive nature of utopia as a place that has no real locality are more interested in its function and effects as a symbol. For

these readers it becomes more important to distinguish between fictional and nonfictional utopias, since this distinction
can play an important role in how a text is read. But, since
these readers, too, construe the relationship between utopian
dream and social reality in different ways, they also reach different conclusions about the effects that literary utopias have
on readers.

Readers like Northrop Frye, for example, see the relationship between dream and reality in terms of mediation
and synthesis. For Frye, the impact of literary utopias is similar to that of a "speculative myth" in that they both provide
the reader with "an imaginative vision of the *telos* or end at
which social life aims."[6] The essential function of such a
myth, according to Frye, is to envision a more integrated image of society, an image purified of social conflicts, tensions,
and discrepancies. By providing us with a harmonious image
of social relations, utopias can help to ease our fears and apprehensions about the social and political tensions that exist
in our society. Read this way, the efficacy of utopias lies in
their capacity to reconcile, on a symbolic level, real social contradictions and antagonisms. As symbolic mediations, utopias can have a therapeutic effect on readers: they supply us
with heuristic models of order, harmony, and fulfillment that
can help us cope more adequately in an imperfect, fragmented, and hostile world.

This urge to reconcile and balance the conflicts within society is indeed a powerful one that can be detected to some
extent in all utopian efforts. It can be traced from More's *Utopia*, which sets out to balance the demands of a newly emerging form of city life with an older, conflicting form of rural
existence, to Huxley's *Island*, which projects a desirable integration of Eastern religion and Western science and technology. But such images of integration and mythlike balance,
as we have seen, are possible only within a closed utopia, a
utopia that is located outside of history. As Huxley's Pala

makes clear, once utopia abandons this privileged position and opens its boundaries to history, its mediating power proves temporary at best and illusory in the long run. From a historical perspective, even these closed and isolated utopias that purport to achieve perfect harmony and balance do not escape social contradictions altogether; indeed, as Marin shows in his reading of More's *Utopia,* these contradictions are invariably reproduced in the utopian figure, where they are critically distanced and made more apparent. In their effort to reconcile social contradictions, then, such integrated utopias as those of More and Huxley also succeed in throwing these contradictions into sharper relief. But this intensification of contradictions will become evident to us only if we approach these texts as speculative interrogations of social possibilities. As "speculative myths," they have a limited impact on readers, providing us with consolations and assurances that allow us to remain in a passive posture.

In short, if we want to uncover the activating potential of utopian literature, we must recognize its experimental nature and its cognitive function as a literature of purposive estrangement. For rather than simply consoling the reader with a perfect version of an imperfect world, a static synthesis that effaces social conflicts and differences, utopias can also be seen to intensify these conflicts in order to stimulate in the reader a desire for social change. This desire emerges from the interplay between social fact and utopian fantasy, an interplay that critically distances and reveals existing social arrangements as arbitrary, provisional, and changeable. Thus, the critical impact of utopian literature moves beyond the provision of a mythlike mediation that may reconcile us to contradictions, to a more active questioning of those contradictions, a questioning that entices us to abandon our old certainties and convictions and to explore alternative possibilities.

The activating potential of literary utopias will be more fully realized, then, if we approach these texts not as symbolic mediations of cultural contradictions but as intensifications of them. For readers like Marin and Suvin, utopias are also symbolic constructs, fictive no-places constructed in hypothetical alternative locations, but for these readers the crucial effect of these symbols is in their power to defamiliarize existing ideology and make it appear "strange." In relating the utopian vision to the social reality it seeks to replace, these readers see the former not as a reassuring myth that relieves us of our social fears and anxieties, but as a disturbing dialectical inversion that arouses our social concern. By stessing the basic incongruity between utopian dream and social reality, these readers draw attention to the distance that separates the two, a distance which, according to Marin, both reveals and conceals the true nature of social reality: utopias reveal the dominant ideology as a form of "false consciousness"; that is, they expose existing social relations as historical and changeable, and then conceal this recognition by denying their own provisional status in the historical process. Read this way, the efficacy of those utopian dreamworlds is not in the feasibility of their designs, nor in their therapeutic effects as heuristic models of peace and perfect harmony, but in their shocking and disturbing effects on readers who are now forced to think about the nature of their own lives and the socioeconomic system in which they live.

This intensely critical method of reading utopias develops a perspective that accounts for their revelatory power and enhances the potentially activating impact they can have on readers. In this perspective, the activity of reading literary utopias is essentially an encounter with the unfamiliar, an imaginary journey to a strange land whose remarkable transformations enable the reader to survey the more familiar territory of history with fresh eyes. Like the traveler to utopia, the reader recognizes this familiar territory as intolerably wasteful, constraining, and arbitrary in its organization, but he also realiz s that it is capable of being changed. Unlike the traveler in the text, however, who is able to leave this wretched world behind and escape into the utopian dream, the reader is left with a sense of uneasiness because this remote and happy region is nowhere, because it is outside of history and experience. On closer inspection, the reader discovers not only that this ostensibly perfect region is incompatible with history, but that it is also less than perfect: there are a number of gaps and inconsistencies that remain in its social, economic, and political structure; its claims of permanence and perfectibility are contradicted by the very revelations it has made about the inescapability of history. Suspended now between this strange land that is nowhere in existence and a familiar land that is extremely constraining and repressive, the reader finds himself, literally, between an intolerable social reality and an impossible social dream. In thus situating the reader between two views of social life that cannot be reconciled, utopias achieve their most productive effect: now all forms of social order and all forms of social relations—utopian and nonutopian—can be seen as tentative and historical, that is, as having been produced by human action and capable of being changed by human action.

This way of interrogating literary utopias shows us how we can unlock potentially greater value from texts generally regarded as "poor ore" once we discard our habit of reading them as blueprints for social action or as perfect mediations of cultural contradictions. Regarded as inconclusive examinations of social contradictions, utopias involve the reader in an activity of his own—a kind of controlled thought-experiment—in which possible variations to social reality can be tried out and entertained. Utopias provide us with the important site where these interrogations can be conducted, a neutral space where oppositions, discrepancies, and inconsistencies can be tested and where identities and differences can be established, at least temporarily. To realize this potential effect of utopias, however, the reader must become more active. Instead of passively accepting or simply rejecting utopian solutions formulated in the text, the reader must question them more critically, attempt to identify what they seek to conceal or repress, and respond by producing utopian variations of his own. Such intense participation by the reader is justified by the dialogical structure upon which utopias are based and by the implicit recognition that utopia is an ongoing process of overcoming historical obstacles, a recognition that utopia is always in the making.

This kind of critical response is, moreover, much more in keeping with the critical vocation of utopias. Utopias generally begin with a fundamental dissatisfaction with the status quo. Their strategy is to demystify existing social patterns and routines by defamiliarizing them and exposing the contradictions inherent in them. In their search for possible variations, they are ready to confront difficult questions and dilemmas: What is a good society? How can we achieve both security and freedom? Is it possible to reconcile individual difference and community? How can we satisfy both the demands for self-realization and the need for communal well-being? These questions pose dilemmas that are in their very nature contradictory and incapable of a permanent solution. Thus, no matter how confidently a utopia may claim to have solved them, a critical reader reading in the dialectical and open-ended spirit reinforced by utopias must resist any permanent answers that these texts may offer.

Some utopias, as we have seen, confront the reader directly with these questions without attempting to provide a conclusive answer. Morson has shown how certain "meta-utopias" break with the programmatic tendency of other, more closed, utopias and rupture their apparent one-dimensionality by speaking to us overtly with two voices—utopian and anti-utopian—neither of which is presented as authoritative in the text. For Morson, however, only a very few texts achieve this

kind of productive resonance, while the great majority of utopias remain one-sided, representations of ideal and perfect
social relations intended for enactment. This is no doubt because, for Morson as for many critics, readers are locked into
reading conventions and habits that determine their response—an essentially passive model of the reader/text relationship. It is to counter such reading habits that the open-
ended utopian narratives of Wells, Piercy, and Le Guin are
intentionally constructed as inconclusive and indeterminate,
thereby forcing the reader to assume a more active role. These
ambiguous utopias give the reader more freedom *and* more
responsibility in producing utopian values and in envisioning
utopian possibilities. In these texts, utopia, as a region of realized happiness, is incomplete, insufficient, or not represented
at all; it is evoked as a genuine no-place. But this explicit shift
in the burden of constructing utopia—from the text to the
reader—constitutes a shift in degree, not in kind—a vigorous
effort to develop the open-endedness that is implicit in the dialectical structure of all utopias.

If we are ready to recognize the critical perspective exemplified by Marin and Suvin as a more productive way of
reading literary utopias, we should nevertheless remain cautious about making anticipatory claims for them, as Marin
does. The view that utopias are able to predict future developments is a view that very few readers of utopias are willing
to defend. Even a cursory survey of past utopias from More
to Bellamy to Stapledon shows that in terms of their predictive power utopias usually fall short of actual developments.[7]
In fairness to Marin, we must note that it is not exactly proph-
ecy he has in mind when he attributes an anticipatory function to utopias. Rather, Marin's reading of More's *Utopia* locates a much subtler form of anticipation in More's text: traces
and foreshadowings of a future that intimate what was inac-
cessible to consciousness at the time the work was composed.
Utopias, in Marin's view, are capable of expressing on a precon-

ceptual level fragments of a future history, but they themselves remain locked in their own time and place. This anticipatory power, therefore, can only come to light subsequently, after a different conceptual framework has been developed which can account for it. Unconscious of this power, according to Marin, utopias (and utopian authors) are "blind" instruments of the historical process that nevertheless manage to catch a glimpse of the changes on the horizon of their own present moment.

This anticipatory function will become apparent, however, only if we accept Marin's ideological priorities as a reader and if we concur with his propensity for reading significance into what other readers may see as minor details in the text. We may of course reject Marin's reading of these unconsciously embedded details in the text; but what is more difficult to reject, and what utopias accomplish on a more conscious level, is the articulation of contradictions in the author's time and place. More's *Utopia* may be read as a remarkable anticipation of socialism (as Marin essentially reads it), or it may be read as a nostalgic glance backward to a monastic form of communal life and cooperation (as other readers have read it). This indicates that More's text is indeterminate, and that different readings of it are possible and, indeed, encouraged by the text. From our perspective today, however, the future that may have been anticipated in More's text, and the past it may have tried to recover, are both historically dated and constitute for us moments that are in the past. I have tried to argue, therefore, that the real interest of More's text, for his sixteenth-century audience of Latin-reading humanists as well as for his present-day audience, is not the subtle anticipation of the future, nor necessarily the glorification of a distant past, but the cognitive defamiliarization of its present moment as a moment in history.

Utopias, in other words, are not so much innovative or anticipatory of the "new" as they are clarifications and illuminations of existing states of affairs. It is in disclosing the present moment as a part of a historical continuum—a past that informs a present and opens up the future—that utopias produce their most important effect on readers: they make us aware that our present situation is inextricably linked to our past and that the future depends on our choices and actions in the present. Thus, instead of providing us with an escape from history—a trip to a never-never land of timeless and consoling ideals—utopias can be seen to put us in closer touch with history; instead of obscuring the gap between social reality and utopian desire, they make this gap more visible. Their most productive effect, then, is to give us a sense of the historicity of social life and to inspire us to envision our own images of the future, images that reinforce the need for human community, shared enterprise, and a common purpose here and now, so that we are able to reach the next stage in history. What makes this effort so urgent is the recognition that Zamyatin's lobotomized robots, Huxley's conditioned, mindless happiness, and Orwell's totalitarian nightmare are also possibilities that we can realize. But such possibilities can be sustained only in a society in which it is no longer possible to imagine that which does not exist—a society that has done away with utopias altogether.

There are tangible signs today indicating that the utopian imagination may be in a period of decline: the utopian promises of the 1960s and 1970s seem to have evaporated; the prospects of nuclear and ecological nightmares have made the future unthinkable; utopian thought and utopian writing are dwindling. Reasons for this decline can be found easily enough, but perhaps the most obvious one is that for most people the future has become a region of fear and dread rather than of hope. The recent past is equally depressing, a story of terror best forgotten or retrieved more comfortably in the form of a television miniseries. Given this general situation, people are understandably apprehensive about any

kind of change. They may be willing to make a few modifications here and there, but only insofar as these modifications
will make the existing system function more smoothly and
more efficiently. In an age of supermarkets, shopping malls,
cable television, fast-food stores, communication satellites,
and an array of different versions of the Sears Roebuck spring
and summer catalog, the whole idea of utopia seems some-
how incongruous and antiquated. Life in a consumer society
is, after all, fairly pleasant: our needs, desires, and aspirations are well-managed and satisfied, including our need for
fantasies and dreams. Have we not reached precisely the kind
of well-being and happiness that those old utopian dreamers
dreamt about? If we are convinced that this is so, then we
have indeed reached the "end of utopia," not because its realization means its inevitable destruction, but because we have
become, like Plato's cave dwellers, prisoners who are blind to
the reality in which we live and unable to understand our
relationship to our own personal and historical futures.

Fortunately, however, there are also tangible signs that the
utopian imagination has not yet disappeared completely.
Pockets of utopian enthusiasm remain and, on occasion,
flourish, as they did in the 1970s. Fictional utopias, like Le
Guin's *The Dispossessed* and Piercy's *Woman on the Edge of Time*,
can be seen as vital signs of a persistent effort to revive the
twofold utopian function of providing a critical diagnosis of
existing social relations and envisioning a liberated alternative. Yet, for the most part, we must nevertheless concede
that today's efforts to revitalize utopian thought seem pale
when compared with those of the past. The essence of utopian thinking has always been a desire for a thorough restructuring of social relations and a radical transformation of social
life. Such a restructuring implies the possibility of a perspective outside of and in opposition to the status quo. In a homogeneous society such as our own, so completely standard-
ized, systematized, and programmed by mass culture, such a

perspective is more and more difficult to achieve. There are simply fewer areas of discontent and fewer remaining dissatisfactions in a society that delivers the goods and provides so many distractions. The net result is that many forms of utopian expression surviving today seem vacuous and lacking in genuine utopian content.

Many futurists, for example, seem content to study the future in order to exploit its economic possibilities. They project patterns of production and consumption—"megatrends"—into a future that is perceived as a more efficient version of the present, rather than entertaining an alternative that challenges it. Similarly, the liberal concept of a "meta-utopia" that Robert Nozick proposes in his study *Anarchy, State, and Utopia* (1974) generously embraces diverse models of utopia in order to accommodate currently held views on individualism and self-interest, rather than questioning the assumptions upon which these views are based. The limitation of these efforts, it seems to me, is that in their failure to provide any genuine opposition to the status quo, they also fail both to defamiliarize the present situation sufficiently and to intensify our perception of it. Instead, they tend to reinforce and confirm values that have been largely co-opted and assimilated by the prevailing ideology. Unable to provide a genuine alternative to existing society, such efforts are unable to generate the critical distance necessary to expose its contradictions. In their critical impact, they are similar to Skinner's *Walden Two*, in which the utopian imagination is reduced to finding a better way to manage and maintain the status quo.

A much more promising direction for the possible revitalization of utopian thought is indicated by those writers and critics for whom utopia implies a negation of the existing structures of society. For writers like Piercy and Le Guin, for critics like Marin and Suvin, as well as for social thinkers like Herbert Marcuse and Ernst Bloch, the efficacy of utopian thought and utopian literature lies in its critical impact on readers—in its power to startle, disturb, and shock the reader and to reorient his or her attitudes. To achieve this effect, utopias must set out to undermine the existing ideology at the same time that they reinforce the ineradicable human desire for happiness and fulfillment; they must make apparent the ways in which existing society inhibits our social possibilities at the same time that they provide some genuine utopian content—the yearning for community, social harmony, more authentic human relationships. For utopia, as we have seen, is not just an ideal vision of the future, nor a blueprint for its realization, but a dialectical method for exploring our limitations and our possibilities, a dialectic that allows us to examine our historical situation with anxiety and hope. The method of this dialectical exploration is unique and its effects can be liberating: utopia displaces social reality with dream, giving us access to the forces of manipulation and domination that constrain us, and invites us to dream our own utopian dreams. The crucial effect of this dialectic is that it enables us to apprehend our own present moment as a moment in history. In defamiliarizing *and* restructuring our perception of the present moment, utopia becomes an index for history itself, our social history as well as our personal history.

Notes

PREFACE

1. *The Order of Things: An Archaeology of Human Sciences* (New York: Pantheon Books, 1970), p. xviii.

2. "Of Islands and Trenches: Naturalization and the Production of Utopian Discourse," *Diacritics* 7 (June 1977), p. 2.

CHAPTER 1. INTRODUCTION

1. For a discussion of the background and history of utopian communities, see Barbara Goodwin and Keith Taylor, *The Politics of Utopia: A Study in Theory and Practice* (New York: St. Martin's Press, 1982), pp. 119–81. Contrary to the view that these communities generally failed to realize their utopian ideals, the authors argue that a number of these experiments were quite successful.

2. For a more detailed discussion of these readings of More's text, see Melvin J. Lasky's *Utopia and Revolution* (Chicago: University of Chicago Press, 1976), pp. 15–18.

3. See Marin's "Toward a Semiotic of Utopia: Political and Fictional Discourse in Thomas More's *Utopia*," in *Structure, Consciousness, and History,* ed. Richard Harvey Brown and Stanford M. Lyman (London: Cambridge University Press, 1978), pp. 261–82.

4. See Kolakowski's essay "The Concept of the Left," in *Toward a Marxist Humanism,* trans. Jane Zielonko Peel (New York: Grove Press, 1979), pp. 69–70.

5. A notable exception was T. H. Huxley, who expressed

what must be one of the most sanguine attitudes toward utopia when he stated that "if some great Power would agree to make me always think what is true and do what is right, on condition of being turned into a sort of clock and wound up every morning before I got out of bed, I should instantly close with the offer. The only freedom I care about is the freedom to do right; the freedom to do wrong I am ready to part with on the cheapest terms to anyone who will take it of me." Quoted in George Kateb's *Utopia and Its Enemies* (New York: Schocken Books, 1972), p. 160.

6. H. G. Wells, *A Modern Utopia* (1905; reprint, Lincoln: University of Nebraska Press, 1967), p. 9.

7. See "Socialism: Utopian and Scientific," in *Essential Works of Marxism,* ed. Arthur P. Mendel (New York: Bantam Books, 1971), pp. 45–82.

8. See, for example, Michael Holquist's argument in his essay "How to Play Utopia: Some Brief Notes on the Distinctiveness of Utopian Fiction," in *Game, Play, Literature* (Boston: Beacon Press, 1971): 106–23.

9. *Utopia* (New York: Harmony Books, 1978). The quotation appears on the cover of the book.

10. *Utopian Fantasy: A Study of English Utopian Fiction Since the End of the Nineteenth Century,* 2d ed. (New York: McGraw-Hill, 1973), p. xiii.

11. *Utopian Thought in the Western World* (Cambridge: Harvard University Press, 1979).

12. The parallel situation of the traveler to utopia and the reader of the utopian text has been analyzed by Gary Saul Morson. See *The Boundaries of Genre: Dostoevsky's "Diary of a Writer" and the Tradition of Literary Utopias* (Austin: University of Texas Press, 1981), pp. 96–104.

13. "Varieties of Literary Utopias," in *Utopias and Utopian Thought,* ed. Frank E. Manuel (Boston: Houghton, 1966), p. 329.

14. *Future Shock* (New York: Bantam Books, 1971), pp. 458–70.

15. *Das Prinzip Hoffnung,* 2 vols. (Frankfurt am Main: Suhrkamp, 1959), p. 180.

16. "Theses on Ideology and Utopia," trans. Fredric Jameson, *Minnesota Review* 6 (Spring 1976), p. 75. (This is a translation of a central chapter in Marin's book *Utopiques: Jeux d'espaces* [Paris: Edition de minuit, 1973].)

17. *The Act of Reading: A Theory of Aesthetic Response* (Baltimore: Johns Hopkins University Press, 1978), p. x.

18. See Eco's *Role of the Reader: Explorations in the Semiotics of Texts* (Bloomington: Indiana University Press, 1979). Eco demonstrates how such "closed" texts as Superman films and James Bond novels are "immoderately 'open' to every possible interpretation" (p. 8).

19. "Defining the Literary Genre of Utopia: Some Historical Semantics, Some Genology, a Proposal, and a Plea," in *Metamorphoses of Science Fiction: On the Poetics and History of a Literary Genre* (New Haven: Yale University Press, 1979), p. 37. (Also published in *Studies in the Literary Imagination* 6 [1973]: 121–45).

20. "How to Play Utopia: Some Brief Notes on the Distinctiveness of Utopian Fiction," p. 109.

21. Marin's semiotic approach to the analysis of utopian narrative will be discussed in detail in chapter 4.

22. The dedication page of Le Guin's utopian novel *The Dispossessed* (Avon Books, 1975) reads "for the partner," which may be read as a reference to her husband but which may also be understood in terms of the collaborative role she has in mind for her readers. For an analysis of this role as Le Guin describes it, see Chapter 6.

23. See Morson's *Boundaries of Genre*, p. 78. (Emphasis in original.)

CHAPTER 2. DISPUTED BOUNDARIES

1. For a discussion of the problematic nature of utopian boundaries, see Fredric Jameson's "Of Islands and Trenches: Naturalization and the Production of Utopian Discourse," *Diacritics* 7 (June 1977), pp. 2–21.

2. Karl Mannheim's *Ideology and Utopia: An Introduction to the Sociology of Knowledge*, trans. Louis Wirth and Edward

Shils (New York: Harcourt, Brace and World, [1936]), defines utopia in terms of a "situation-transcending" idea that unmasks what the prevailing ideology seeks to conceal. Mannheim also provides a taxonomy of four basic types of utopias along political lines: chiliastic, liberal-humanitarian, conservative, and Socialist-Communist. Popper's critique is in his *Open Society and Its Enemies,* 3d ed., 2 vols. (London: Routledge and Kegan Paul, 1957). For a fair-minded discussion of the arguments for and against utopian thinking see George Kateb's *Utopia and Its Enemies* (New York: Schocken Books, 1972).

3. See Polak's *Image of the Future* (New York: Oceana, 1961) and his *Prognostics* (New York: Elsevier, 1971).

4. *Future Shock* (New York: Bantam Books, 1971), p. 463.

5. "Toward More Vivid Utopias," *Science* 126 (1957), p. 961.

6. "In Defense of Utopia," *Ethics* 65 (1955), p. 135.

7. See especially Marcuse's *Essay on Liberation* (Boston: Beacon Press, 1969), p. 48, and Paul and Percival Goodman's *Communitas: Means of Livelihood and Ways of Life* (New York: Vintage, 1960).

8. *The Politics of Utopia: A Study in Theory and Practice* (New York: St. Martin's Press, 1982), p. 58.

9. *Utopian Thought in the Western World* (Cambridge: Harvard University Press, 1979).

10. *The Shape of Utopia* (Chicago: University of Chicago Press, 1970), p. 110.

11. Gary Saul Morson, *The Boundaries of Genre: Dostoevsky's "Diary of a Writer" and the Traditions of Literary Utopia* (Austin: University of Texas Press, 1981), p. 69. (Hereafter cited within the text.)

12. The complete title of Suvin's essay is "Defining the Literary Genre of Utopia: Some Historical Semantics, Some Genology, a Proposal, and a Plea," in *Metamorphoses of Science Fiction: On the Poetics and History of a Literary Genre* (New Haven: Yale University Press, 1979), pp. 37–62. (Also published in *Studies in the Literary Imagination* 6 [1973], pp. 121–45.) (Further citations to this and other essays in *Metamorphoses* will be carried in the text.)

13. Frye places utopias within the form and tradition of the anatomy (which emphasizes dissection and analysis) and, more specifically, within Menippean satire which, according to Frye, "presents us with a vision of the world in terms of a single intellectual pattern" (p. 310). The essential features of both are an interest in "abstract ideas and theories," a form that is "stylized rather than naturalistic," and an overall orientation that "deals less with people as such than with mental attitudes" (p. 309). See Frye's *Anatomy of Criticism* (Princeton: Princeton University Press, 1957), pp. 308–12.

14. *The Republic of Plato*, trans. Francis MacDonald Cornford (1941; reprint, New York: Oxford University Press, 1968), p. 110.

15. For a detailed description of Iser's theory of aesthetic response, see *The Act of Reading* (Baltimore: Johns Hopkins University Press, 1978). The interplay between reader and text is discussed at length on pages 163–231. (Subsequent citations to this work will be carried in the text.)

16. "The Reading Process: A Phenomenological Approach," in *The Implied Reader: Patterns of Communication in Prose Fiction from Bunyan to Beckett* (Baltimore: Johns Hopkins University Press, 1974), p. 287.

17. Barthes's famous distinction between "writerly" and "readerly" texts, as is often pointed out, is based not so much on properties in the text as it is on different reading strategies: the "readerly" approach considers the text as closed and determinate, while the "writerly" approach sees the text as "a galaxy of signifiers; it has no beginning; it is reversible; we gain access to it by several entrances, none of which can be authoritatively declared as the main one." See Barthes's *S/Z*, trans. Richard Miller (New York: Hill and Wang, 1974), p. 5.

18. See Wells's *Modern Utopia* (Lincoln: University of Nebraska Press, 1967), pp. 208–9.

CHAPTER 3. THE ROLE OF THE READER

1. As defined by William K. Wimsatt and Monroe C. Beardsley, "The Affective Fallacy is a confusion between the

poem and its results. . . . It begins by trying to derive the standard of criticism from the psychological effects of a poem and ends in impressionism and relativism." *The Verbal Icon: Studies in the Meaning of Poetry* (Lexington: University Press of Kentucky, 1967), p. 21. Reader-oriented critics would argue, of course, that a poem or any work of art cannot be understood apart from its results or its "effects" on readers.

2. For a survey of the various reader-oriented approaches and the diverse models of the reader/text relationship, see *The Reader in the Text*, ed. Susan B. Suleiman and Inge Crosman (Princeton: Princeton University Press, 1980), and *Reader-Response Criticism*, ed. Jane P. Tompkins (Baltimore: Johns Hopkins University Press, 1980).

3. For a critical and historical account of the various approaches that "reception aesthetics" entails, see Peter U. Hohendahl's essays "Introduction to Reception Aesthetics," *New German Critique* 10 (Winter 1977), pp. 29–63, and "Beyond Reception Aesthetics," *New German Critique* 28 (Winter 1983), pp. 108–46.

4. Iser's model of "the implied reader" is described in his *Act of Reading: A Theory of Aesthetic Response* (Baltimore: Johns Hopkins University Press, 1978), pp. 34–38 (subsequent citations to this work will be carried in the text), and in the chapter "The Reading Process: A Phenomenological Approach," in *The Implied Reader: Patterns of Communication in Prose Fiction from Bunyan to Beckett* (Baltimore: Johns Hopkins University Press, 1974), pp. 274–94. Eco's "Model Reader" is elaborated in his "Introduction: The Role of the Reader," in *The Role of the Reader: Explorations in the Semiotics of Texts* (Bloomington: Indiana University Press, 1979), pp. 3–43. This collection of Eco's writings on this subject also contains his important essay "The Poetics of the Open Work," pp. 47–66.

5. Representative essays by Fish and Bleich can be found in *Reader-Response Criticism*, ed. Jane Tompkins (Baltimore: Johns Hopkins University Press, 1980).

6. *Looking Backward* (New York: Modern Library, 1951). Citations to this work will be carried in the text.

7. See Morson's *Boundaries of Genre*, p. 96.

8. "Theses on Ideology and Utopia," trans. Fredric Jameson, *Minnesota Review* 6 (Spring 1976), p. 71

9. *Fundamentals of Language* (The Hague: Mouton, 1956), p. 76.

10. *The Shape of Utopia* (Chicago: University of Chicago Press, 1970), p. 24.

11. See *Ideology and Utopia,* trans. Louis Wirth and Edward Shils (New York: Harcourt, Brace and World, [1936]), p. 192. (First published in German in 1929.)

CHAPTER 4. MORE'S *Utopia*

1. For a discussion of Hexter's readings see Melvin J. Lasky, *Utopia and Revolution* (Chicago: University of Chicago Press, 1976), pp. 15–18.

2. J. H. Hexter, "Intention, Words, and Meaning: The Case of More's *Utopia*," *New Literary History* 6, no. 3 (Spring 1975), p. 541.

3. C. S. Lewis, "A Jolly Invention," in *Utopia,* trans. and ed. Robert M. Adams (New York: W. W. Norton, 1975), p. 219. Originally published in Lewis's *English Literature in the Sixteenth Century Excluding Drama,* vol. 3 of *The Oxford History of English Literature* (Oxford: Clarendon Press, 1954).

4. Robert M. Adams, "The Prince and the Phalanx" in *Utopia,* trans. and ed. Robert M. Adams (New York: W. W. Norton, 1975), p. 203. See also Russel Ames, *Citizen Thomas More and His Utopia* (Princeton: Princeton University Press, 1949), pp. 8–21.

5. "Theses on Ideology and Utopia," trans. Fredric Jameson, *Minnesota Review* 6 (Spring 1976), pp. 71–75.

6. See Marin's "Disneyland: A Degenerate Utopia," *Glyph: Johns Hopkins Textual Studies* 1 (1977), pp. 50–66. For Marin, Disneyland represents a degenerate counter-utopia which functions more like a myth—fixed, permanent, reified— rather than the "play" of opposites which identifies utopia.

7. "Toward a Semiotic of Utopia: Political and Fictional Discourse in Thomas More's *Utopia,* in: *Structure, Consciousness, and History,* ed. Richard H. Brown and Stanford M. Lyman

(London: Cambridge University Press, 1978), p. 271. Subsequent references will be carried in the text.

8. All references to More's *Utopia* are to the edition of Edward Surtz, S. J. (New Haven: Yale University Press, 1964), p. 24.

9. Bertrand Russell, *A History of Western Philosophy* (New York: Simon and Schuster, 1963), p. 522.

10. Readers of *Utopia* have put forth different arguments over the years as to which voice in the text is authoritative. If Thomas More speaks through "More," then Hythloday becomes a somewhat dangerous character whose views must be rejected; if More speaks through Hythloday, then "More" is a "gull" or a protective device that allows More to express his own subversive political views. For a discussion of these readings see Robert C. Elliott's *The Shape of Utopia: Studies in a Literary Genre* (Chicago: University of Chicago Press, 1970), pp. 25–49.

11. Darko Suvin, *Metamorphoses of Science Fiction*, p. 91.

CHAPTER 5. THE ANTI-UTOPIA

1. For a reconsideration of "Socialism: Utopian and Scientific," see the special supplement "Marxism and Utopia," *Minnesota Review* 6 (Spring 1976), pp. 52–139.

2. *The Shape of Utopia* (Chicago: University of Chicago Press, 1970), p. 89.

3. See *Eros and Civilization* (New York: Vintage Books, 1962) and *One-Dimensional Man* (Boston: Beacon Press, 1964).

4. For an analysis of the impact of *Looking Backward*, see Jean Pfaelzer, "Parody and Satire in American Dystopian Fiction of the Nineteenth Century," *Science-Fiction Studies* 7 (March 1980), pp. 61–71.

5. Although the terms "anti-utopia" and "dystopia" are generally used interchangeably to designate those works that satirize and parody utopian ideals, critics have often attempted to draw important distinctions between them. Morson, for example, defines dystopia as "a type of anti-utopia that discredits

utopias by portraying the likely effects of their realization, in contrast to other anti-utopias which discredit the possibility of their realization or expose the folly and inadequacy of their proponents' assumptions or logic." *The Boundaries of Genre,* p. 116. Thus, a dystopia inverts the "good-place" into a "bad-place," whereas anti-utopia embraces a more general negative orientation toward utopian goals.

6. "Of Islands and Trenches: Naturalization and the Production of Utopian Discourse," *Diacritics* 7 (June 1977), p. 3.

7. Pfaelzer, "Parody and Satire in American Dystopian Fiction of the Nineteenth Century," p. 61.

8. *We* was written in 1920–1921. Rejected for publication in the Soviet Union, the book first appeared in English translation in 1924 and in Czech translation in 1927. The first Russian edition was published, apparently without Zamyatin's knowledge, in an émigré journal in Czechoslovakia. Denounced at the meeting of the Writer's Union in 1929, Zamyatin was unable to publish in the Soviet Union and requested permission to leave. His request was granted in 1931. He spent his remaining years in Paris, where he died of heart disease in 1937. For further information on the publishing history of *We,* see Mirra Ginsburg's introduction to the Bantam edition.

9. Robert C. Elliot, *The Shape of Utopia,* pp. 97–98.

10. *Nineteen Eighty-Four* (1949; reprint, New York: New American Library, 1950), p. 220.

11. *Brave New World* (1939; reprint, New York: Bantam Books, 1953), p. 163.

12. Quotes are from Mirra Ginsburg's introduction to *We,* trans. Mirra Ginsburg (New York: Bantam Books, 1972), p. xi. Further citations are to this edition.

13. "Of Man's Last Disobedience: Zamiatin's *We* and Orwell's *1984,*" *Comparative Literature Studies* 10, no. 4 (December 1973), p. 286.

14. Fyodor Dostoevsky, *The Brothers Karamazov,* trans. Constance Garnett (New York: New American Library, 1958), p. 233.

15. Olaf Stapledon, *Last and First Men* (1930; reprint, London: Penguin Books, 1976), p. 12.

CHAPTER 6. THE AMBIGUOUS UTOPIA

1. Bülent Somay, "Towards an Open-Ended Utopia," *Science Fiction Studies* 11 (March 1984), p. 26.

2. See Eco's *Role of the Reader* (Bloomington: Indiana University Press, 1979), pp. 9–10.

3. *A Modern Utopia* (Lincoln: University of Nebraska Press, 1967), p. 11. Subsequent citations are to this edition and will be carried in the text.

4. Morson defines "meta-utopias" as "examinations, rather than endorsements or rejections, of the presuppositions of utopian thinking and literature." See *Boundaries of Genre* (Austin: University of Texas Press, 1981), p. 146. Robert Nozick has argued for the value of "meta-utopias" in providing a more comprehensive perspective that avoids the pitfalls of making specific utopian proposals. "Half the truth I wish to put forth," he writes, "is that utopia is meta-utopia." See *Anarchy, State, and Utopia* (New York: Basic Books, 1974), p. 312. Although I share the view that a modern utopia must necessarily encompass a meta-utopian perspective on utopian values, my own interests are in determining the kinds of effects that this broader perspective has on readers.

5. For a thoughtful discussion of the range of open-endedness reflected in recent utopian narrative, see the essay by Bülent Somay cited above. I am indebted to a manuscript reader for referring me to this article, which reaches conclusions similar to my own.

6. Aldous Huxley, *Brave New World* (1939; reprint, New York: Bantam Classic, 1953), p. viii.

7. Aldous Huxley, *Island* (New York: Bantam Books, 1963). Originally published by Harper and Row in 1962.

8. Huxley's description of those who would inhabit the hypothetical "third alternative." See *Brave New World,* p. viii.

9. *Walden Two* (New York: Macmillan Company, 1948), pp. 174 and 111.

10. See, for example, Andrew Hacker's essay "Dostoevsky's Disciples: Man and Sheep in Political Theory," *Journal of Politics* 17 (1955), pp. 590–613.

11. See, for example, Joseph Wood Krutch's attack of *Walden Two* as "an ignoble utopia which describes the contented life led by inmates of an institution." *The Measure of Man* (New York: Harcourt Brace, 1954).

12. *Ecotopia: The Notebooks and Reports of William Weston* (New York: Bantam Books, 1975), p. 55.

13. *Woman on the Edge of Time* (New York: Ballantine Books, 1976), p. 328.

14. This subtitle, which appeared in the hardcover edition published by Harper and Row in 1974, was inexplicably left off the title page of the Avon paperback edition. It does, however, appear on the front cover of the book. *The Dispossessed* (New York: Avon Books, 1975).

15. Ursula K. Le Guin, *The Language of the Night: Essays on Fantasy and Science Fiction*, ed. Susan Wood (New York: G. P. Putnam's Sons, 1979), p. 127. In his essay "You, U. K. Le Guin," Norman Holland provides an excellent example of the reader as active collaborator by responding to various thematic and structural gaps in Le Guin's novel *The Left Hand of Darkness*. Holland describes the open-endedness of the novel in terms of "a constant reaching out for completion" (p. 137) and carries on a dialogue with the author in which he traces "a theme of completing the incomplete through every phase of this novel." "Your novel," Holland addresses the author directly, "exists as a novel only as I—or someone else—makes it a novel. It is like a child, dependent for its very existence on an other; and, oddly, its final character will result from, will *be* the complex interaction of tale and hearer" (p. 135, emphasis in original). Holland's essay appears in *Female Futures: A Critical Anthology*, ed. Marleen S. Barr (Bowling Green, Ohio: Bowling Green State University Popular Press, 1981): 125–37.

16. "Is Gender Necessary?" in *The Language of the Night*, p. 163.

17. "Introduction to *The Left Hand of Darkness*," in *The Language of the Night*, p. 156.

18. "World-Reduction in Le Guin: The Emergence of Utopian Narrative," *Science-Fiction Studies* 3 (November 1975), p. 223.

19. Nadia Khouri, "The Dialectics of Power: Utopia in the Science Fiction of Le Guin, Jeury, and Piercy," *Science-Fiction Studies* 7 (March 1980), pp. 54–55.

CHAPTER 7. CONCLUSION

1. Louis Marin, "Theses on Ideology and Utopia," trans. Fredric Jameson, *Minnesota Review* 6 (Spring 1976), p. 71.

2. Quoted in Marie Louise Berneri's *Journey Through Utopia* (New York: Schocken Books, 1971), p. 308.

3. Jost Hermand, "The Necessity of Utopian Thinking," *Soundings* 58 (Spring 1975), pp. 97–111.

4. See, for example, Kathleen Kincade's *Walden Two Experiment: The First Five Years of Twin Oaks Community* (New York: William Morrow, 1973), which details the struggles, successes, and failures of an experiment based on Skinner's *Walden Two*. For a description of the various "utopian" experiments in communal living during the 1960s and 1970s see Ron Roberts, *The New Communes* (Englewood Cliffs: Prentice Hall, 1971).

5. *Utopiques: Jeux d'espaces* (Paris: Edition de minuit), p. 351.

6. "Varieties of Literary Utopias," in *Utopias and Utopian Thought*, ed. Frank E. Manuel (Boston: Houghton, 1966), p. 323.

7. Frye, for example, writes, "The technological utopia has one literary disadvantage: its predictions are likely to fall short of what comes true, so that what the writer saw in the glow of vision we see only as a crude version of ordinary life." See "Varieties of Literary Utopias," p. 328.

Bibliography

Amis, Kingsley. *New Maps of Hell: A Survey of Science Fiction.* New York: Ballantine, 1960.

Bakhtin, Mikhail M. *The Dialogic Imagination.* Edited by Michael Holquist and translated by Caryl Emerson and Michael Holquist. Austin: University of Texas Press, 1981.

Barthes, Roland. *The Pleasure of the Text.* Translated by Richard Miller. New York: Hill and Wang, 1975.

_____. *Sade, Fourier, Loyola.* Translated by Richard Miller. New York: Hill and Wang, 1976.

_____. *S/Z.* Translated by Richard Miller. New York: Hill and Wang, 1974.

Beauchamp, Gorman. "Of Man's Last Disobedience: Zamiatin's *We* and Orwell's *1984.*" *Comparative Literature Studies* 10, no. 4 (December 1973): 285–301.

_____. "Themes and Uses of Fictional Utopias: A Bibliography of Secondary Works in English." *Science-Fiction Studies* 4 (1977): 55–63.

_____. "Utopia and Its Discontents." *Midwest Quarterly* 16 (1975): 161–74.

Bellamy, Edward. *Looking Backward: 2000–1887.* 1887. Reprint. New York: Random House, Modern Library, 1951.

Berneri, Marie Louise. *Journey Through Utopia.* 1950. Reprint. New York: Schocken Books, 1971.

Bevington, David M. "The Dialogue in *Utopia:* Two Sides to the Question." In *More's "Utopia" and Its Critics,* edited by Ligeia Gallagher, 160–70. Chicago: Scott, Foresman, 1964.

Bierman, Judah. "Science and Society in the *New Atlantis* and Other Renaissance Utopias." *PMLA* 10 (1963): 492–500.

Bleich, David. *Subjective Criticism*. Baltimore: Johns Hopkins University Press, 1978.

Bloch, Ernst. *Geist der Utopie*. 2d ed. Frankfurt am Main: Suhrkamp, 1964.

———. *A Philosophy of the Future*. Translated by John Cumming. New York: Herder and Herder, 1970.

———. *Das Prinzip Hoffnung*. 2 vols. Frankfurt am Main: Suhrkamp, 1959.

Booth, Wayne C. *The Rhetoric of Fiction*. Chicago: University of Chicago Press, 1961.

Bowman, Sylvia E. "Utopian Views of Man and the Machine." *Studies in the Literary Imagination* 6 (Fall 1973): 105–20.

Buber, Martin. *Paths in Utopia*. Translated by R. F. C. Hull. Boston: Beacon Press, 1958.

Callenbach, Ernest. *Ecotopia: The Notebooks and Reports of William Weston*. 1975. Reprint. New York: Bantam, 1977.

Campanella, Tommaso. *The City of the Sun: A Poetical Dialogue*. Translated by Daniel J. Donno. Berkeley and Los Angeles: University of California Press, 1981.

Culler, Jonathan. *On Deconstruction: Theory and Criticism After Structuralism*. New York: Cornell University Press, 1982.

———. *The Pursuit of Signs: Semiotics, Literature, Deconstruction*. New York: Cornell University Press, 1981.

Dostoevsky, Fyodor. *The Brothers Karamazov*. Reprint. Translated by Constance Garnett. Edited by Manuel Komroff. New York: New American Library, Signet Classic, 1958.

Eco, Umberto. *The Role of the Reader: Explorations in the Semiotics of Texts*. Bloomington: Indiana University Press, 1979.

Elliott, Robert C. *The Shape of Utopia: Studies in a Literary Genre*. Chicago: University of Chicago Press, 1970.

Engels, Friedrich. "Socialism: Utopian and Scientific." In *Essential Works of Marxism*, edited by Arthur P. Mendel, 45–82. New York: Bantam Books, 1961.

Fekete, John. "*The Dispossessed* and *Triton*: Act and System in Utopian Science Fiction." *Science-Fiction Studies* 6 (1979): 129–43.

Fish, Stanley E. *Is There a Text in This Class? The Authority of Interpretive Communities.* Cambridge: Harvard University Press, 1980.

Foucault, Michel. *The Order of Things: An Archaeology of the Human Sciences.* Translated by Alan Sheridan-Smith. New York: Pantheon Books, 1970.

Frye, Northrop. *Anatomy of Criticism.* Princeton: Princeton University Press, 1957.

_____. "Varieties of Literary Utopias." In *Utopias and Utopian Thought,* edited by Frank E. Manuel, 323–47. Boston: Houghton Mifflin, 1966.

Gerber, Richard. *Utopian Fantasy: A Study of English Utopian Fiction Since the End of the Nineteenth Century.* 2d ed. New York: McGraw-Hill, 1973.

Goodman, Paul, and Percival Goodman. *Communitas: Means of Livelihood and Ways of Life.* 2d ed. New York: Random House, Vintage Books, 1960.

Goodwin, Barbara, and Keith Taylor. *The Politics of Utopia: A Study in Theory and Practice.* New York: St. Martin's Press, 1983.

Grimm, Reinhold, and Jost Hermand. *Deutsches utopisches Denken im 20. Jahrhundert.* Stuttgart: W. Kohlhammer, 1974.

Hacker, Andrew. "In Defense of Utopia." *Ethics* 65 (1955): 135–38.

_____. "Dostoevsky's Disciples: Man and Sheep in Political Theory." *Journal of Politics* 17 (1955): 590–613.

Hermand, Jost. "The Necessity of Utopian Thinking." Translated by Janet King and Betty Weber. *Soundings* 58 (Spring 1975): 97–111.

Hertzler, Joyce Oramel. *The History of Utopian Thought.* New York: Macmillan, 1923.

Hexter, J. H. "Intention, Words, and Meaning: The Case of More's *Utopia.*" *New Literary History* 6, no. 3 (Spring 1975): 529–41.

Hill, Eugene D. "The Place of the Future: Louis Marin and His *Utopiques.*" *Science-Fiction Studies* 9 (1982): 167–79.

Hohendahl, Peter U. "Beyond Reception Aesthetics." Translated by Philip Brewster. *New German Critique* 28 (Winter 1983): 108–46.

———. "Introduction to Reception Aesthetics." Translated by Marc Silberman. *New German Critique* 10 (Winter 1977): 29–63.

Holland, Norman N. *The Dynamics of Literary Response.* New York: Oxford University Press, 1968.

———. "You, U. K. Le Guin." In *Future Females: A Critical Anthology,* edited by Marleen S. Barr, 125–37. Bowling Green: Bowling Green State University Popular Press, 1981.

Holquist, Michael. "How to Play Utopia: Some Brief Notes on the Distinctiveness of Utopian Fiction." In *Game, Play, Literature,* edited by Jacques Ehrmann, 106–23. Boston: Beacon Press, 1971.

Huntington, John. "Utopian and Anti-Utopian Logic: H. G. Wells and His Successors." *Science-Fiction Studies* 9 (1982): 122–46.

Huxley, Aldous. *Brave New World.* 1939. Reprint. New York: Bantam Books, 1953.

———. *Island.* 1962. Reprint. New York: Bantam Books, 1963.

Iser, Wolfgang. *The Act of Reading: A Theory of Aesthetic Response.* Baltimore: Johns Hopkins University Press, 1978.

———. *The Implied Reader: Patterns of Communication in Prose Fiction from Bunyan to Beckett.* Baltimore: Johns Hopkins University Press, 1974.

———. "Indeterminacy and the Reader's Response in Prose Fiction." In *Aspects of Narrative,* edited by J. Hillis Miller, 1–45. New York: Columbia University Press, 1971.

———. "Interaction Between Text and Reader." In *The Reader in the Text: Essays on Audience and Interpretation,* edited by Susan R. Suleiman and Inge Crosman, 106–19. Princeton: Princeton University Press, 1980.

Jakobson, Roman. "Two Aspects of Language and Two Types of Aphasic Disturbances." In *Fundamentals of Language.* The Hague: Mouton, 1956.

Jameson, Fredric. *Marxism and Form: Twentieth-Century Dialectical Theories of Literature.* Princeton: Princeton University Press, 1971.

_____. "Introduction/Prospectus: To Reconsider the Relationship of Marxism to Utopian Thought." *Minnesota Review* 6 (1976): 53–58.

_____. "Of Islands and Trenches: Naturalization and the Production of Utopian Discourse." *Diacritics* 7 (June 1977): 2–21.

_____. "Progress Versus Utopia; or, Can We Imagine the Future?" *Science-Fiction Studies* 9 (1982): 147–58.

_____. "World-Reduction in Le Guin: The Emergence of Utopian Narrative." *Science-Fiction Studies* 2 (1975): 221–30.

Jauss, Hans Robert. *Literaturgeschichte als Provokation.* Frankfurt am Main: Suhrkamp, 1970.

Kateb, George. *Utopia and Its Enemies.* 1963. Reprint. New York: Schocken Books, 1972.

_____, ed. *Utopia.* New York: Atherton Press, 1971.

Ketterer, David. *New Worlds for Old: The Apocalyptic Imagination, Science Fiction, and American Literature.* Bloomington: Indiana University Press, 1974.

Khouri, Nadia. "The Dialectics of Power: Utopia in the Science Fiction of Le Guin, Jeury, and Piercy." *Science-Fiction Studies* 7 (March 1980): 49–60.

Kolakowski, Leszek. "The Concept of the Left." In *Toward a Marxist Humanism,* translated by Jane Zielonko Peel, 67–83. New York: Grove Press, 1969.

Krutch, Joseph Wood. *The Measure of Man.* New York: Harcourt Brace, 1954.

Krysmanski, Hans-Jürgen. *Die utopische Methode: Eine Literatur- und wissensoziologische Untersuchung deutscher utopischer Romane des 20. Jahrhunderts.* Cologne: Westdeutscher Verlag, 1963.

Lasky, Melvin J. *Utopia and Revolution.* Chicago: University of Chicago Press, 1976.

Le Guin, Ursula K. *The Dispossessed.* 1974. New York: Avon Books, 1975.

_____. *The Language of the Night: Essays on Fantasy and Science Fiction.* Edited by Susan Wood. New York: G. P. Putnam's Sons, Perigee Books, 1979.

——. *The New Atlantis*. In *The New Atlantis and Other Novellas of Science Fiction*, edited by Robert Silverberg, 65–93. New York: Warner Books, 1975.

Mailloux, Steven J. "Reader-Response Criticism?" *Genre* 10 (Fall 1977): 413–31.

Mannheim, Karl. *Ideology and Utopia: An Introduction to the Sociology of Knowledge*. Translated by Louis Wirth and Edward Shils. New York: Harcourt, Brace and World, [1936]. (First published in German in 1929.)

Manuel, Frank E., and Fritzie P. Manuel. *Utopian Thought in the Western World*. Cambridge: Harvard University Press, 1979.

——, eds. *French Utopias: An Anthology of Ideal Societies*. 1966. Reprint. New York: Schocken Books, 1971.

Manuel, Frank E., ed. *Utopias and Utopian Thought*. Boston: Houghton, 1966.

Marcuse, Herbert. *Eros and Civilization: A Philosophical Inquiry into Freud*. 1955. Reprint. New York: Random House, Vintage Books, 1962.

——. *An Essay on Liberation*. Boston: Beacon Press, 1969.

——. *One-Dimensional Man: Studies in the Ideology of Advanced Industrial Society*. Boston: Beacon Press, 1964.

——. "The End of Utopia." In *Five Lectures: Psychoanalysis, Politics, and Utopia*, translated by Jeremy J. Shapiro and Shierry M. Weber. Boston: Beacon Press, 1970.

Marin, Louis. *Utopiques: Jeux d'espaces*. Paris: Edition de minuit, 1973.

——. "Disneyland: A Degenerate Utopia." *Glyph* 1 (1977): 50–66.

——. "Theses on Ideology and Utopia." Translated by Fredric Jameson. *Minnesota Review* 6 (Spring 1976): 71–75.

——. "Toward a Semiotic of Utopia: Political and Fictional Discourse in Thomas More's *Utopia*." In *Structure, Consciousness, and History*, edited by Richard Harvey Brown and Stanford M. Lyman, 261–82. London: Cambridge University Press, 1978.

———. "Toward a Theory of Reading in the Visual Arts: Poussin's *The Arcadian Shepherds.*" In *The Reader in the Text: Essays on Audience and Interpretation,* edited by Susan R. Suleiman and Inge Crosman, 292–324. Princeton: Princeton University Press, 1980.

Mead, Margaret. "Toward More Vivid Utopias." *Science* 126 (1957): 957–61.

Molnar, Thomas. *Utopia: The Perennial Heresy.* New York: Sheed and Ward, 1967.

More, Thomas. *Utopia.* Edited by Edward Surtz, S.J. New Haven: Yale University Press, 1964.

Morris, William. *News from Nowhere.* 1891. Reprint. Edited by James Redmond. London: Routledge and Kegan Paul, 1970.

Morson, Gary Saul. *The Boundaries of Genre: Dostoevsky's "Diary of a Writer" and the Traditions of Literary Utopia.* Austin: University of Texas Press, 1981.

Moylan, Tom. "The Locus of Hope: Utopia Versus Ideology." *Science-Fiction Studies* 9 (1982): 159–66.

Mumford, Lewis. *The Story of Utopias: Ideal Commonwealths and Social Myths.* New York: Boni and Liveright, 1922.

Negley, Glenn Robert. *Utopian Literature: A Bibliography with a Supplementary Listing of Works Influential in Utopian Thought.* Lawrence: The Regents Press of Kansas, 1977.

Negley, Glenn Robert, and J. Max Patrick. *The Quest for Utopia: An Anthology of Imaginary Societies.* New York: Henry Schuman, 1952.

Nelson, William, ed. *Twentieth-Century Interpretations of "Utopia."* Englewood Cliffs, N.J.: Prentice Hall, 1968.

Neusüss, Arnhelm, ed. *Utopie: Begriff und Phänomen des Utopischen.* Neuwied: Luchterhand, 1968.

Nozick, Robert. *Anarchy, State, and Utopia.* New York: Basic Books, 1974.

Orwell, George. *Nineteen Eighty-Four.* 1949. Reprint. New York: New American Library, Signet, 1950.

Pfaelzer, Jean. "Parody and Satire in American Dystopian Fiction of the Nineteenth Century." *Science-Fiction Studies* 7 (March 1980): 61–71.

Philmus, Robert M. "The Language of Utopia." *Studies in the Literary Imagination* 6 (Fall 1973): 61–78.

Piercy, Marge. *Dance the Eagle to Sleep.* 1970. Reprint. New York: Ballantine Books, Fawcett Crest Book, 1982.

———. *Woman on the Edge of Time.* 1977. Reprint. New York: Ballantine Books, Fawcett Crest Book, 1983.

Plato. *The Republic of Plato.* 1941. Reprint. Translated with introduction and notes by Francis MacDonald Cornford. New York: Oxford University Press, 1968.

Polak, Frederik Lodewik. *The Image of the Future.* 2 vols. Leiden and New York: Oceana, 1961.

Popper, Karl R. *The Open Society and Its Enemies.* 3d ed., 2 vols. London: Routledge and Kegan Paul, 1957.

Riesman, David. "Some Observations on Community Plans and Utopia." *Yale Law Journal* 57 (1947): 173–200.

Ruppert, Peter. "Utopian Thinking: Old Limitations and New Possibilities." *Southern Humanities Review* 11 (Fall 1977): 337–45.

Ruyer, Raymond. *L'Utopie et les utopies.* Paris: Presses Universitaires de France, 1950.

Sargent, Lyman Tower. "Themes in Utopian Fiction Before Wells." *Science-Fiction Studies* 3 (1976): 275–82.

———, ed. *British and American Utopian Literature, 1516–1975: An Annotated Bibliography.* Boston: G. K. Hall, 1979.

Schlanger, Judith E. "Power and Weakness of the Utopian Imagination." Translated by Mary Burnet. *Diogenes* 84 (1973): 1–24.

Shklovsky, Victor. "Art as Technique." In *Russian Formalist Criticism: Four Essays,* edited and translated by Lee T. Lemon and Marion J. Reis, 5–24. Lincoln: University of Nebraska Press, 1955.

Skinner, B. F. *Walden Two.* New York: Macmillan, 1948.

Somay, Bülent. "Towards an Open-Ended Utopia." *Science-Fiction Studies* 11 (March 1984): 25–38.

Suleiman, Susan R., and Inge Crosman, eds. *The Reader in the Text: Essays on Audience and Interpretation.* Princeton: Princeton University Press, 1980.

Suvin, Darko. *Metamorphoses of Science Fiction: On the Poetics and History of a Literary Genre*. New Haven: Yale University Press, 1979.

———. "Defining the Literary Genre of Utopia: Some Historical Semantics, Some Genology, a Proposal, and a Plea." In *Metamorphoses of Science Fiction*, 37–62. First published in *Studies in the Literary Imagination* 6 (Fall 1973): 121–45.

———. "Parables of De-Alienation: Le Guin's Widdershins Dance." *Science-Fiction Studies* 7 (1980): 265–74.

———. "'Utopian' and 'Scientific': Two Attributes for Socialism from Engels." *Minnesota Review* 6 (Spring 1976): 59–70.

———. "Utopian Tradition of Russian Science Fiction." *Modern Language Review* 66 (1971): 139–59.

Tillich, Paul. *Politische Bedeutung der Utopie für das Leben der Völker*. Berlin: Weiss, 1951.

Todd, Ian, and Michael Wheeler. *Utopia*. New York: Harmony Books, 1978.

Todorov, Tzvetan. *The Fantastic: A Structural Approach to a Literary Genre*. Translated by Richard Howard. New York: Cornell University Press, 1975.

Toffler, Alvin. *Future Shock*. 1970. Reprint. New York: Bantam, 1971.

Tompkins, Jane P., ed. *Reader-Response Criticism: From Formalism to Post-Structuralism*. Baltimore: Johns Hopkins University Press, 1981.

Tuveson, Ernest Lee. *Millennium and Utopia: A Study of the Background of the Idea of Progress*. New York: Harper and Row, 1964.

Walsh, Chad. *From Utopia to Nightmare*. London: Geoffrey Bles, 1962.

———. "Attitudes Toward Science in the Modern 'Inverted Utopia.'" *Extrapolation* 2 (1961): 23–26.

Weinkauf, Mary S. "Edenic Motifs in Utopian Fiction." *Extrapolation* 11 (1969): 15–22.

Wells, H. G. *A Modern Utopia*. 1905. Reprint. Lincoln: University of Nebraska Press, 1967.

Williams, Raymond. "Utopia and Science Fiction." *Science-Fiction Studies* 5 (1978): 203–14.

Woodcock, George. "Utopias in Negative." *Sewanee Review* 64 (1959): 81–97.

Zamyatin, Yevgeny. *We*. Translated by Mirra Ginsberg. New York: Bantam Books, 1972.

Index